*We dedicate this book to all those children
who have gone through divorce—
and to all those who will.*

Don't Divorce Us!

Kids' Advice to Divorcing Parents

Rita Sommers-Flanagan
Chelsea Elander
John Sommers-Flanagan

ACA
AMERICAN
COUNSELING
ASSOCIATION

DON'T DIVORCE US! KIDS' ADVICE TO DIVORCING PARENTS

10 9 8 7 6 5 4 3 2 1

American Counseling Association
5999 Stevenson Avenue
Alexandria VA 22304

Director of Publications
Carolyn C. Baker

Copy Editor
Wendy Lieberman Taylor

Cover design by BonoTom Studio

Library of Congress Cataloging-in-Publication Data
Sommers-Flanagan, Rita, 1953–
    Don't divorce us! : kids' advice to divorcing parents / by Rita
Sommers-Flanagan, Chelsea Elander, John Sommers-Flanagan.
      p. cm.
    Includes bibliographical references.
    ISBN 1-55620-175-3 (alk. paper)
    1. Children of divorced parents—United States Interviews.
2. Children of divorced parents—United States—Family relationships.
3. Adult children of divorced parents—United States—Interviews. 4. Adult
children of divorced parents—United States—Family relationships.
5. Divorce—United States—Psychological aspects. 6. Divorced people— United
States—Family relationships. I. Elander, Chelsea. II. Sommers-Flanagan,
John,1957– III. Title.
HQ777.5.S6 1999
306.89—dc21   99-40492
                                           CIP

Table of Contents

Acknowledgments

First and foremost, we offer thanks to our hundreds of anonymous co-authors who took the time to offer their advice to divorcing families. You know who you are, even if no one else does, and we are deeply indebted to each of you. You boldly shared your insights, with simple words, and were always captivating. We hope we did justice to what you offered.

Next we thank those who scurried around gathering essays and interview participants on our behalf: Robin Hamilton, Joyce Hannula, Rick Hannula, Peggy Lotz, Julie Parker, John Reynolds, Kevin Wallace, Dan Wilcox, Sarah Baxter, and Sam Maniar.

We are indebted to the Montana State University Honors College student grant for funding a part of the time Chelsea spent gathering advice, which helped the dream begin to take shape.

Our reviewers, Susan Simonds and Elizabeth Welfel, offered support, excellent suggestions, and a vision of what this book might become. Our editor, Carolyn Baker, as always, was a superb source of help and encouragement.

To the extended family—Eric, Terri, Midge, Jim, Paula, Max, and Mary Lou—thank you for daring to break the old molds. It's been worth it. And finally, we offer thanks and love to Rylee, who has been patient, supportive, funny, kind, and wise beyond her years while the rest of her family wrote a book.

About the Authors

Rita Sommers-Flanagan is a clinical psychologist and professor of counseling at the University of Montana. In her professional practice, Rita has often worked as both a counselor and a mediator for divorcing or remarried families. She and John are co-authors of *Tough Kids, Cool Counseling* and *Clinical Interviewing*. For 16 years, Rita has been part of a four-parent team, with lots of grandparents, aunts, and uncles thrown in, devoted to raising the second author, Chelsea. So far, the formula seems to have worked. In fact, it worked so well that the same team often helps out with Rita and John's 11-year-old daughter, Rylee. Rita and Chelsea have talked about writing this book for the past 15 years. They finally did it, and they still like each other.

Chelsea Elander is a 22-year-old senior at Montana State University. She is the biological daughter of Rita Sommers-Flanagan and Eric Elander and the stepdaughter of Terri Elander and John Sommers-Flanagan. As a child of divorce, Chelsea learned early in her life how to pack all of life's little essentials into one small suitcase. Besides her packing abilities, Chelsea's accomplishments include earning a Montana State University Presidential Scholarship, Junior Woman of the Year award, selection to a *USA Today* All-Academic Team, and a Truman Scholarship. She is grateful for the diverse perspectives and many lessons learned from all her parents, except perhaps what John taught her to do in the event of a victory in a family game. In a recent news profile of Chelsea, she stated, "I'm honored to get these awards, but the credit goes to my four parents and my incredible family." Her younger sister, Rylee, who was watching the show, stated, "Wow, I hope I get her genes!"

Dr. John Sommers-Flanagan is a clinical psychologist, executive director of Families First Parenting Programs in Missoula, Montana, and Chelsea's stepfather. He is also an author, newspaper columnist, and nationally recognized speaker and workshop instructor. One of his many professional interests is helping divorcing families. John appreciates the fact that Rita and Chelsea allowed him to help write this book, despite the fact that he has made one or two notorious errors in his stepfathering efforts. Fortunately, these errors do not seem to have had lasting negative effects on Chelsea, other than her rather aversive tendency to leap to her feet and march around the room with upraised arms whenever she emerges victorious from friendly family competitions.

Introduction

Families come in an amazing variety of sizes, styles, and configurations: single-parent families, two-parent families, adoptive families, extended families, childless families, and multigenerational families. There are aunts and uncles raising children, grandparents raising children, and foster parents raising children. Many religious and community leaders, social scientists, and politicians believe the family is the basis of society and that healthy families are the centerpiece of a healthy community. However, families are not static, reliable, immutable entities. They are in constant flux. Children are born, grow up, and depart from their families of origin (often returning and leaving again several times!). Adult relationships, commitments, and needs change, often necessitating changes in the family structure.

As Alvin Toffler pointed out in his book *Future Shock*, change is the rule in human existence, not the exception. Change is the rule in the life of the family, too. We rarely have a choice about whether change will happen, but we have many choices about how to respond to the changes that come into and define our families and our lives.

Divorce is an obvious and dramatic change in the life of a family. Estimates vary, but even the most optimistic reports indicate that between a third and a half of all marriages will end in divorce. It is a rare individual who has not, in some way, been affected by a divorce at some point in his or her life—whether by having parents or grandparents divorce, by having friends with divorced parents, by teaching

1

or working with divorced people or children of divorce, by a spouse's prior divorce, or by being divorced him- or herself.

Social scientists have conducted many studies on the causes and effects of divorce. A confusing array of books exist on the topic. Mental health professionals specialize in couples counseling, custody evaluations, and adjustment-to-divorce groups or individual work. Yet, with all this studying and writing and counseling, many people feel we are still causing more damage than we need to when couples with children divorce. So we decided to contribute to that confusing array of books, and write one ourselves—but we wanted hundreds of co-authors. Instead of summarizing scientific studies or expounding on our professional opinions, we decided to listen to the people who have been there—the children of divorce—and let their input guide the writing of this book.

HOW WE GOT THE INPUT

We have four main sources for the contents of this book. First, we interviewed volunteers personally, in one-on-one, tape-recorded sessions, and transcribed what they had to say. Chelsea conducted many of the interviews. Second, as clinical psychologists, John and Rita have worked with all sorts of families going through divorce, which certainly influenced us and our contributions to the book. Third, we solicited essays, artwork, e-mails, and input from all over the country through advertising, by contact with other professionals, and by word of mouth. Our final source of information is personal—we've been there ourselves and thereby have our own thoughts on the matter. Chelsea is a child of divorce, Rita is a divorced parent, and John is a stepparent. The divorce happened when Chelsea was five years old. John became her stepfather when she was almost eight. These direct, personal experiences with divorce and with being a blended family have necessarily shaped and informed our worldview and added to our motivation for writing this book.

Throughout the book, we have used actual quotes from children and adult children of divorce. Some of the quotes are used word for word. Others have been edited and paraphrased to capture the essence of the communication. A few actual essays in the handwriting of the respondents and some original artwork are included to give you the flavor of these candid, humorous, and profoundly touching contributions.

We have disguised every response so that no real names, locations, or other identifying factors have been used. Sometimes, but not always, age and sex of those quoted or discussed have also been altered. We have not identified the ethnicity, religious affiliation, or race of any respondent in particular. Although the majority of our respondents reported themselves to be from White, middle-class backgrounds, we had a number of American Indian, Hispanic, Asian American, Russian, and African American respondents. We also had first-generation immigrant respondents and a few who identified themselves as having mixed racial and ethnic backgrounds. A large number of Judeo-Christian religious orientations were represented, including students from two high school classes from a private Catholic school. Thanks to e-mail and the American Counseling Association's publication, *Counseling Today*, we had a wonderfully comprehensive range of geographic locations in the United States represented. With all this diversity and the deliberate disguises, anyone believing they know a person we've quoted will probably be wrong.

We had a number of enthusiastic respondents who were quite willing to have us identify them, but it seemed wiser to have a policy of anonymity. Generally, this allows for a freer expression of thoughts and feelings and reduces the chances of accidentally or intentionally hurting anyone. For over 2 years, we talked with all ages of people— whoever we found who wanted to talk. As you who are social scientist types will quickly surmise, this is *not* a scientific study. We simply gathered up the advice and input of people who've been there and wove it together. However, it comes as no surprise that their advice aligns quite closely with most of the more scholarly divorce outcome and parenting literature. We mention some of these sources in chapter 8.

WHOSE SIDE ARE WE ON, ANYWAY?

This book is unabashedly one-sided. We're completely on the side of the children. We want their voices to shine through and speak to divorcing parents on the deepest possible level. Our bias is that being a parent or a stepparent is a privilege and a huge responsibility. Neither good parenting nor good stepparenting is something that comes naturally. Certainly, some people seem better at it than others, but all parents and stepparents can learn and improve. One way to improve is to listen very closely to the needs and longings and advice these voices of experience have to offer.

HUMANLY IMPOSSIBLE?

As we looked over the essays and talked with the children of divorce, a great irony became apparent. The things the children were saying seemed straightforward, reasonable, and full of common sense. Their requests and guidance seemed simple enough. But the truth is, the children's advice condensed and recorded in this book might be the hardest advice any parent ever tries to follow. Both personally and professionally, we are aware that the breaking apart of a committed romantic relationship is a trauma of immense proportions and usually encompasses complicated, ongoing, severe consequences.

Most divorces are replete with feelings of betrayal, pain, and defeat. When we are hurt, we want to hurt back. We want to get even. We even want revenge. There's hardly any worse hurt than that of a broken love promise. When we feel defeated, we lose our sense of self-worth and self-efficacy. People in this situation often experience self-loathing, shame, rage, loneliness, fear, disgust, and even hatred—it's as if divorcing people fall into a bottomless pit of extremely difficult emotions. And it's rare for things ever to get easy again between divorced people. We're not saying it can't happen, but it's unusual.

If no children were produced or involved, the two joined lives can come apart and the individuals can begin the healing process. Even then, it isn't a simple process. But if you add in children, the healing gets very challenging. The relationship-loss wound can all too easily be chronically reopened by the needs of the children. When children are a part of a divorcing family, they are a graphic, constant, physical reminder of all that could have been, all that was, and all the pain. They remind us of our own failure and hurt. They remind us of the one who failed or hurt us. And—here's the irony—if we do it right, the children keep us tied quite closely to the person we just divorced.

THE WRONG QUESTION

Often, people search for someone to blame when things go wrong. In *Life's Little Instruction Book*, the 1991 book by H. Jackson Brown, instruction number 354 says, "To explain a romantic break-up, simply say, 'It was all my fault.'" That's not bad advice. To take it one step further, it may be best to stop asking the question "Who's to blame here?" That question is impossible to answer anyway, and attempting to assign blame does not promote healing. In all likelihood, both adults made plenty of mistakes and therefore have an abundance of opportunities to grow, change, and heal.

Of course, none, absolutely *none*, of the divorce is the children's fault. They didn't ask the parents to get together, and they didn't ask to be born. They are vulnerable, dependent beings who desperately need mature, stable, loving parents. They may have presented certain difficulties and challenges to their parents, but their parents are the adults responsible to address the difficulties and challenges. If, for whatever reason, the adult relationship cannot be sustained, it isn't the children's fault.

The back of a local pediatric dentist's card has this saying: "Children are the only known substance from which adults can be formed." What a wonderful challenge—and what an ominous warning. For the children's sakes, certainly, but for our society's sake as well, we need to find ways to give children the love and stability they need, even if their parents cannot stay married. This book is intended to help you who are divorcing parents hear what children need from you. It is intended to rattle and disturb and challenge. It is intended to give you vision, compassion, and courage.

Attending to children's needs while going through a divorce is an enormous obligation. Sorting out how to raise healthy, happy children while you are co-parenting with someone who divorced you or whom you divorced is a monumental task. We hope the following chapters will help. Read on, and listen to the voices of the children.

CHAPTER 1

Preparing for Divorce

Marriages, like families, are unique. People looking in from the outside of these committed relationships do not have the right to determine if or when they should end. Many couples face difficult times, betrayals, or personal changes that lead them to question the viability of their intimate relationship.

To the best of our knowledge, healthy marriages with two loving, mature parents (and a lot of nice relatives and neighbors) provide the very finest possible situation for raising children. The jury is still out on exactly how adverse and long lasting the effects of a less healthy marriage are on particular children. It is certainly quite possible that a good divorce is better for children than a bad marriage. One of our respondents, an 18-year-old girl, said,

"My parents' divorce was essential—it had to take place for the survival of my family."

Another began the essay he wrote for us with the following,

"Please let me say first that I am very grateful for my parents' divorce. I shudder when I think about the picture I would have had of marriage, gender roles, gender relationships, sex, and family had they stayed together."

And we read this, from a 16-year-old girl:

"The environment before they finally split was horrible. They would fight nonstop so much that sometimes I just hated even

7

being home. That wasn't fair that I couldn't be in my own home and feel comfortable."

Some children found especially creative ways to tell us about their experience of being in a dysfunctional family or of going through a divorce. For instance, a budding rap star shared his thoughts on his parents' bad marriage in the following poem:

Bad Marriage Blues

Young girl says to her mom,
How did you know that father was the one?
Her mom just rolls her eyes.
She says, you'll find that special guy.
But to herself she cannot lie....

Do you take this woman?
I don't.
Do you take this man?
I don't.
For the rest of your awful life
She is your lawful wedded wife
Eternal agony, this holy matrimony.

Difficult, dysfunctional marriages can make home feel more like a war zone. They can make children feel frightened, disgusted, and disconnected from the rest of the apparently happy world. Ten-year-old Tanner wrote,

"My mom and dad fought a lot, and they both seemed mean when they were together. I guess it was all the anger about not getting along. I could hear them fighting all the time, and I hated it. Now that they are divorced, life at home is kinder and calmer. We get along better."

Unhappy parents are not as likely to be available to their children in healthy ways, but they may be tempted to use their children to hide from their marital troubles. Children can feel they've been asked to take sides or to fill in where a parent has withdrawn.

Bad marriages can, and undoubtedly do, give children less than ideal role models for their own dating and marriage attitudes and behaviors. Some children worry that they will end up with someone who will make them as unhappy as their parents seem. Others swear they will never venture forth and take the risk of making a commitment. Still others report that they have promised themselves they will find a mate who is exactly the opposite of their parents. Certainly, staying in a relationship that is hurtful and unloving can be destructive in many ways for everyone involved.

On the other hand, divorce has been described as one of the most stressful things a human being can face. Deciding to divorce is a very adult and often a very private matter. Children should never be directly consulted or given decision-making power regarding whether a divorce proceeds or not. The desire to protect the children and meet their needs is a large part of what makes the decision to divorce so difficult and complicated. Certainly, they can be informed and listened to, but children should not ever be given the final say.

THE MISERABLY UNDECIDED

When people get married, they almost always believe they are making a lifelong commitment to live faithfully with each other. They pledge to stay together, to love and honor each other through good times and bad times. Very few people can break such a commitment without serious soul-searching, sadness, and mixed feelings. However, this indecision can be a wrenching time for the children and the extended family.

The children we interviewed, especially those who had recently been through it, expressed impatience with this ambivalence. Kyle, a 9-year-old boy whose parents had talked about getting a divorce for years, said,

> *"I think that parents thinking about a divorce should either know what they want or forget about it. Either go through with it or don't. It's the in-between that is hard on kids and everyone."*

Josh, a 17-year-old honors student, said,

> *"You know, I think I cared, way back when, if they got divorced or not. But I'm sick of it now. My dad has moved out three times. My mom, once. My brother has learned to manipulate them both. He's 13 and already has about everything money can buy. They say they are trying to work it out for us, but you know, I*

think it's the money or the status or something. I've told them to just get it over. We didn't used to say that, but anything would be better than this."

There's no question that indecision and marital ambiguity are hard on all family members. Almost everyone is more comfortable with a predictable future. From a child's perspective, even a week is a considerable length of time. Although it is most certainly a bad idea to rush into a divorce decision, there are things parents can do to make this time more tolerable for the children. Many of our respondents advised parents to let their children know the basics of what is being considered and to know how long they might be expected to wait to hear a decision. During this undecided time, children especially don't want to become pawns in the decision-making process. Often, children told us about dreading the bitterness, hostility, and parent-child manipulations that they anticipated as a part of the divorce decision-making process.

One wise 12-year-old girl shared this:

"My parents' divorce is going on right now. So far, it has been as friendly as divorce can be, but I think once it comes down to my mom serving him with the papers, and dividing up property, it could get bitter. Right now, my dad is trying to get my mom back, so he's being nice. When my mom makes it official, it will be a different story. Don't make kids feel guilty for spending time with the other parent, no matter what is going on between you."

Troubled relationships that were once loving relationships are very confusing for children to witness. Change is frightening. Parents who believe they may be heading for divorce need time to sort through their options. They need time to think, try out alternatives, talk, counsel, and do whatever else seems important. Generally children will do better if parents keep them informed and have honest, but nonaccusatory talks about the state of the marriage and efforts to save or end it. From what our interview participants told us, this would be welcomed by most kids. It can be a simple explanation like this: "Jill, you know that your father and I have been thinking we may not want to stay married. And we get pretty upset and confused about it. We're taking some time to think it through and we're seeing a counselor about it. We're really sorry that this makes things hard for you sometimes. We'll try our best to make our marriage healthy again, and you can ask us anything you'd like while we're working on things."

Though difficult, our respondents assured us that gentle, nonblaming honesty is what they want. Sandy, a 13-year-old girl, told us,

"You should always be open and truthful with your children. Parents teach their kids to tell the truth, and they tell them the consequences won't be so bad if they're honest. If that is so, then parents should set a good example and do the same. Your kids are involved in your divorce no matter how you want to look at it. Their family is being broken up because of your divorce. You should treat them with respect and keep them filled in. It may be hard for kids to deal with at first but the overall outcome is a lot better that way."

The kind of honesty children need is the kind that does not ask them or give them permission to take sides. Of course, children will ask unnerving questions such as "Why don't you love Mom anymore?" or "Who's having the affair?" or "Don't you guys love us kids enough to stay together?" These kind of questions deserve careful, reasoned responses. Parents should avoid giving their children long, involved answers that might hurt or confuse them. Instead, work hard to keep the children informed in ways they can understand. Do not pull them into the battle in any way. The words of this 12-year-old girl show how closely children watch, wonder, and surmise:

"My parents divorce is different day by day. It has been 2 years since it started and not a thing has changed in the court. One day it is super nice and the next day it is nasty. It all depends on my dad's mood and what is going on at his work. I don't think my mom wants the divorce. But she feels she has to because of all the things he has done to her. I have no more advice because I need a lot of it myself."

In the absence of clear information about the divorce, children will construct their own ideas about who wants the divorce, who doesn't want the divorce, why their parents are divorcing, and all of the other considerations. Usually, this will not be an accurate picture, and it will lack the balance and comfort that can be offered if parents are clear and honest with their children in sensitive, loving, nonaccusatory ways. We revisit this theme a number of times in later chapters.

OVERT HOSTILITY

Divorcing parents are often hostile with each other. Some of our respondents clearly knew about violence in the home. Their advice was offered at the survival level, directly to the kids. One 11-year-old boy offered,

"Kids need to realize to stay out of the way when parents fight. When they are fighting, kids should go to their room and take the phone. Also, don't hit the wall with your foot and don't get very upset."

Very similar and direct advice came from a 10-year-old girl:

"Kids, if you can't stand the fighting, go outside or to your room. Stay out of the way when your parents fight. Parents, you shouldn't hit in the same room kids are. You shouldn't even hit."

The following essay, featured in original form on page 13, came to us in the mail. It made us determined to write this book and write it well.

"When your parents get divorced, I think that most of the time kids get scared and sometimes cry or scream and that can make the parents maybe take out their anger on the kids. Or make your parents yell at each other more. Some kids may think that the dad might hurt the mom. If you could find a way to prevent that, I would buy that book and talk to my divorced parents."

Hostile, angry, violent parents frighten and hurt their children and need serious professional intervention to help them stop such destructive behaviors.

The most common and most damaging mistake parents make in a difficult marriage is losing control and fighting in front of the children. Things are so tense and awful that parents make snide remarks, or scream and yell, or cry hysterically, or strike out violently. They act in ways that they would never want their children to act, and then later they are ashamed of themselves.

Whin your parents get divorced I think that most of the time kids gets cared and some times cry or scream and that can make the parents mabey take out there anger out on the kids or make your parents yell at each other more. Some kids may think that the Dad might hert the mom.

If you could find a wheay to Prevent that I would by that book and talk to my divorced-Parents.

"My mom moved out when I was seven. Their relationship really started affecting me before that though. I think that I was way more affected by living with my parents' fighting than by the actual separation. I had to do first grade twice because I wasn't paying attention in school. I was worried about what was going on at home when I was gone. When we were home, my brother and I would hear them fighting and we would hide upstairs, my older brother waiting for the time that he thought he should call the police."

This young man's parents' relationship was extremely dysfunctional and abusive. His preoccupation with the turmoil at home was significant enough that his parents and teachers felt he needed to repeat first grade. This is a typical example of how divorce drains children's coping reserves. Human beings have limited amounts of coping energy. Turmoil and hostility at home gobble up enormous amounts of a child's emotional, physical, and intellectual energy, so they don't have much left over to devote to school, friendships, hobbies, lessons, or even household chores. Another child, age 15, offered,

"I remember my dad was always sad and crying and feeling sorry for himself and making life miserable for the rest of us once the possibility of separation was brought up, and I hated it. It was awful. My mom did a very good job of always being calm and sane about it all though. So whatever affects the parents affects the kids at least the same amount, I think. If not the same, then more. It's kind of like a chain reaction."

Fighting parents can also pit siblings against one another, allowing the dissolution of their marriage to bring down the entire family as well. Trisha was 5 years old when her dad left.

"I remember all of the yelling; I always took my dad's side, and my sister always took my mom's side. Now my sister lives with my mom and I have only seen her a few times in the summer."

Conflict is very likely to be present in all human relationships, but it is expressed in a wide variety of ways. Overt hostility, disrespect, cruelty, and violence are terrible for anyone to witness, but they are especially damaging for the dependent children of those involved. You owe it to your children to seek healthy, respectful ways to solve conflicts and to put aside damaging impulses when the children are present. Striking out at the other parent is also a strike at the children. It does no good, solves no problems, and causes great fear and pain in the children.

Social scientists don't often unanimously agree with each other, but on this topic, they do. The evidence is incontrovertible. Children who are exposed to hateful, verbally or physically abusive, contentious, or mean-spirited fighting between their parents suffer greatly from that exposure. Opinions among researchers differ regarding the effects of divorce because there are so many circumstances of divorce. But there are simply no differences of opinion about overt hostility, disrespect, and violence. Those behaviors hurt your children, and in some cases, may leave lasting scars.

The nigh my parent actually separated
My screams were so loud our niebors
thought there was a robberat our
house. When my parents divorced
I went to therapy for 3 years.
This summer I'm going to
Visit my dad for a month and a
weeks.
Bye

Overt hostility also damages the adults involved. As stress and conflict mount, acting out continues, and sometimes, parent conflict erupts into violence or suicide. A sixth-grade boy wrote the following:

"During the divorce before us kids knew they fought loudly all the time and we did not know why. Then one night my dad tried to kill himself by taking all the medicine that he could find."

Many children stated what should seem like common sense, but apparently needs to be mentioned anyway:

"I think that parents should talk about the divorce and that it is going to happen because my parents didn't even talk about it. They also should not throw things, yell, or break things."

And from a 17-year-old boy we heard:

"The most important things while going through a divorce are to keep fights and arguments away from the kids and never bad mouth the other parent in front of anyone."

The consensus among our respondents was loud and clear: Parents, please don't fight in front of us and please don't let us hear you say nasty things about each other. Leave us out of your battles.

THE "STUFF-IT" STYLE

This next section involves, in a sense, the exact opposite problem. Sometimes parents who don't love each other any more do not fight at all. They simply go through the motions of life together, acting polite, calm, or even considerate, while inside they are disengaging from each other. Also, sometimes parents themselves don't even realize how far they have grown apart until something happens and suddenly, the marriage is over. Nine-year-old Maria told us,

"My parents' divorce was awful because I was so shocked this happened. My parents never fought or anything, so I didn't think anything like that could ever happen."

Another child of divorce said,

"I think the main task parents have is to teach their children to love, even in tough times. Love means working things out, not burying them. If there isn't any love, you fight or you bury things."

As a general rule for healthy, happy family life, communication and emotional expression are necessary in liberal doses. Taking time to share how life is going and taking time to listen to each other is basic to sound, nurturing relationships. Still, it is possible to go on for years, living together but relating very little to one another. Children survive such environments, but they do not necessarily thrive. Most want to know what's going on with their parents, together and individually.

"My parents divorced when I was five. My little sister was only one. I have this faint memory of my dad packing and leaving. That's all. I didn't comprehend what was happening. I didn't have a clue. I think they could have talked to me. Even just a few sentences."

Mia, the author of that quote, was an active, curious, verbal child when she was 5 years old. She could have easily understood the basic truth that her family was going to change drastically. No one said a word to her until after her family had actually come apart.

A surprising number of times, our respondents told us of this type of memory: Mystery. Lack of preparation. Shock and amazement. A 59-year-old woman told us that as a 6-year-old girl, she wandered around town looking for her daddy. He had moved into another part of town and she did not actually see him for 7 years. That didn't stop her from looking. Her parents had not gotten along well, but divorce was a very rare thing in those days. When it happened, no one told her it was happening. No one told her why; her father just disappeared. This lack of completion or understanding can plague children for years to come.

An account from a 50-year-old professional woman echoes this theme:

"To this day I can remember how my older brother, younger sister and I learned of the divorce. It was October 13th at 7:00 p.m. in Momma and Daddy's bedroom, where we were called together to talk about Momma and Daddy not loving each other anymore. They were not going to live together anymore. Daddy would be moving out within a few days and we would stay with Momma. Each of my siblings and I felt so violated and so frightened. We cried for most of the evening. That night, we asked each other what we had done to cause the divorce and what we could do to keep Momma and Daddy together."

Some people are not naturally quiet, conflict-avoiding people, but they hold strong beliefs that children should not witness any type of disagreement. They exercise a great deal of control over their emotional responses most of the time. With the best intentions, they try to shield their children from the disagreements and pain. Parents choose to swallow their anger, pride, or sadness completely whenever the kids are in sight or earshot. If not taken to an extreme, modeling emotional control is a good thing for our children.

On the other hand, something is missing when a family allows children to approach a divorce with complete naivete. When parents are so good at hiding their feelings that the announcement of the divorce is a complete shock, the child is set up for a period of disbelief and a skewed picture of how a relationship works or does not work and how a marriage ends. Brian, who was in the seventh grade when his parents got divorced, thought that they were playing some kind of sadistic joke on him.

"No kidding. I honestly didn't even believe them. When they told me, I thought they were just flipping me shit."

Brian had never seen his parents fight, and still, 6 years later, holds the belief that they could have worked it out. It simply didn't make sense to him. They had kept their civil veneer firmly in place, even though when the time came, they assured him (calmly, of course) that they absolutely couldn't stand the idea of staying married.

Other dangers arise from this careful plan to keep kids entirely away from parental problems. Troubled families that are successful in keeping children in the dark most likely have an overall family style that is highly conflict avoidant. The parents have not learned to disagree in thoughtful or respectful ways and have therefore been unable to teach their children how to engage in healthy disagreements. Any hint of conflict sends everyone into hiding. Difficulties are brushed under the rug and smiles are pasted on faces. Differences of opinion are not discussed, disappointments in each other are not shared, and negative feelings are stuffed inside. This is not a particularly good family style under any circumstances, but in the divorcing family, such silence enables the divorce to catch the children by surprise, worsening their shock, deepening their disbelief, and failing to allow them to understand anything about the dynamics that led to the split.

Another problem with conflict avoidance is that children are not usually completely fooled. It is easier to fool or distract younger children; however, as children get older and more able to understand nonverbal signals, they know something is not going well, but they are confused and left to their own interpretations. They have not been given permission to ask about things and have no good role models for talking about feelings or dealing with conflict.

Rosie, who had just graduated from high school when we talked with her, remembers the month before her parents told her and her sisters that they were going to get a divorce. Her parents had been careful to disagree only in private, but Rosie has sensed something was wrong. For instance, she noticed her parents taking long walks, which they never done before, and they did not seem to be affectionate walks. When the family was planning out their summer schedule she was bewildered by the fact that although her mom and dad both had made plans for the summer, they had made separate plans. Her father was not going to her mother's class reunion and her mother was not going to her father's family reunion.

Another new development was her parents' sleeping arrangements. As she was growing up, Rosie had often asked if she could sleep in her parents' bed.

"It used to be a big hassle, but that last month my dad was just like, 'sure,' and he slept on the couch. He was almost glad to have an excuse to be away from my mom. It felt really strange."

Rosie thought of writing her mother a note asking if she was getting a divorce and dropping it off on her desk at work but she couldn't bring herself to do it. So she spent a month aware of the changes but unsure what she was really facing. She was afraid to ask and didn't want her assumptions to be true, but deep down she understood that the potential for divorce was there, and she was confused and frightened.

As Rosie offered her advice for parents thinking about divorce she was very clear that parents should tell the truth to their children as things are being worked out. Rosie was an observant 13-year-old at the time of the divorce. Her parents failure to communicate with her felt like a passive sort of lie. As she said,

"The worst thing was not knowing and not daring to ask. It was all I could think about. They could have sat down and talked to us. It wasn't very nice of them to leave us out like that and in a way, it was like not telling the truth when we most needed them to tell us."

Often kids are far more perceptive than their parents realize. They are tuned into the norms of the household and into the behaviors and feelings their parents display, even if the parents believe otherwise. Another child stressed,

"Don't lie to the children! Most parents tell white lies to their children during a divorce thinking they are helping them cope, but sooner or later, the children find out and eventually won't have as much respect as you want."

Stuff-it style families engender fear and confusion in children when serious dysfunction is occurring. In and of itself, fear is a difficult emotion. When the fear a child is experiencing is fear of the unknown, and the unspoken family rules do not allow for either asking about difficulties or expressing emotions, it is a triple whammy. It is hard to explain marital conflict, loss of love, or plans to divorce to children, but a well thought out, developmentally sensitive talk with the children will help them cope with the realities and stop fearing things that are not true.

THE GIFT OF BALANCE

Parents reading these first two sections may feel confused. First, the children say, "Don't fight in front of us." Then they say, "And don't hide the conflicts." Is it possible to do both? The answer is: not without serious resolve to strike a balance between covered conflict and explosive conflict. The fact is, most of us have trouble with moderation. When conflict occurs, it is easier to either yell or be silent. Books like *Getting to Yes* by Urey, Fischer, and Patton, or *Interpersonal Conflict* by Hocker and Wilmot, are helpful for people who have not been raised with any good role models for dealing with conflict. Sometimes couples counseling or communication classes can be of great help as well. Basically, the important thing is to acknowledge that conflicting values, goals, and habits are present even in the best relationships. It is not shameful or sinful to be angry or hurt or sad regarding how a relationship is going, and at times, it is appropriate for parents to let their children see that they are struggling in the relationship.

"Perhaps my experience was quite different from most people's, but the whole experience of divorce went very smoothly. I think the most important element was that my well-being and happiness was top-priority to both my parents. They also never screamed and yelled even though they disagreed. Actually, they're still friends. I mean, they don't go out to coffee or anything, but they always stayed on good terms."

The 14-year-old boy who shared these thoughts is proud of the way his parents handled their divorce. As a consequence, he can express his feelings about it openly and coherently. He also told us that he feels close to each of his parents.

If parents find ways to share their differences honestly and respectfully with their children, they provide the children with healthy role models and important information. It is not easy for children to know that their parents are having trouble getting along, but if that is the truth of the matter, then it is easier for them to know facts than to be kept in the dark, trying to guess what's wrong.

Some people might object to keeping children up to date regarding family conflicts, saying, "Well, there's no need to scare children unnecessarily. It's better to keep the trouble quiet, hoping the parents can work it out so the kids need never know." Our interview participants, by and large, would strongly disagree. Children want to be told the truth, gently and nonjudgmentally, and want a chance to express their reactions. They need role models for conflict and they need and want to know that their parents did not just get divorced on a whim. They need to know when their parents are facing tough times but are choosing to work on things through talking, counseling, praying, retreats, or whatever means possible. Regardless of the outcome, this knowledge will give children tools for relationship work they will need later and it will help them understand more of why their parents do what they do.

One adult woman whose parents divorced when she was 10 years old shared the following advice:

"Do make a commitment to the children's well-being, and do this with your children present. Agree to be respectful and supportive of one another in regards to child rearing, visitation, and support."

Many of our informants stressed how essential it is to keep children informed. As a 12-year-old girl stated,

"Just because we are kids doesn't mean we don't know what's going on. Ignoring your kids or pretending it is not happening is a bad way to deal with the situation."

One child explained how good it felt to be told about the impending divorce and to be protected from the actual nastiness. Her family was able to protect her with the help of extended family. She was sent to stay with her grandparents while the details of the divorce were worked out. Her parents explained that they were just too stressed out and distressed to give her the kind of attention they wanted to give her. Her grandparents were wonderful, easy to talk to, and supportive:

"The sanctuary of my grandparents' home was my saving grace."

She explained that her grandparents did not take sides and lavished love and care on her during a very difficult time.

Divorce is a painful, difficult experience for parents. Perhaps for some, it is too much to expect that they could be sane, rational, loving parents throughout the process. Using friends, family, or caring church or social communities to surround children and help care for them can be a very welcome addition to the process. Nonetheless, there is no substitute for direct, open communication between parents and children. The following advice was offered by an astute young man whose parents divorced when he was 13 years old:

"I feel parents who are currently getting a divorce need to be open. Parents who are divorcing need to listen to their own children almost more than their present spouse. Because, I mean, think about it...you are going to spend more time in your life with your children than with the person you are about to divorce. The parents need to try and understand. The problem with divorce is that most parents are forcing a very emotional and powerful experience on their children that they, themselves, haven't ever been through. I feel the worst part about my parents' divorce is that they never asked me how I felt about it. They just assumed that I was okay with it and didn't want to talk about it."

Children are, by nature, egocentric. They think they affect the world much more than they do, and they think much of it revolves around them. Unfortunately, this belief often leads to children assuming blame when things aren't going well in their families. Over and over again, divorcing parents need to make sure they take this advice, offered by a 9-year-old boy:

"You should try to get your kids to understand that it's not their fault. When my family was separated, I felt like half my life was getting torn away and that I would never be happy again. But my parents say that they will still be friends and that they both will see us equally."

All of the recent divorce literature tells parents to make sure children understand that divorce is not their fault, but as we have found, this is easier said than done. One small group of youngsters, ages 5 to 8 years, were asked to close their eyes and respond with hand signals to a series of questions. The first question was, "Are you to blame for your parents' divorce?" All five signaled thumbs down, meaning "definitely not." The next question was, "If you had tried a little harder, do you think you could have helped your parents save their marriage?" Most signaled thumbs up, indicating that yes, indeed, they could have tried harder and maybe saved the marriage.

Simply telling the children, "Don't worry, it isn't your fault," is not enough. They need to hear it in a lot of ways, and discuss it at length. They need to know there is nothing at all they could have done to save their parents' marriage.

It is certainly difficult to know how much to communicate and when to communicate. It is hard to figure out how to say things in a balanced, loving way. It is painful to be the bearer of bad, scary news. But remember the basics, which are captured succinctly in this boy's advice:

"Never forget to tell your kids you love them, and never put them in the middle of your problems."

HONESTY AS LOVE; HONESTY AS WEAPON

None of our respondents indicated they wanted their parents to lie to them. They wanted open, honest, respectful communication about what was happening. The art of telling someone you love difficult truths is not terribly well developed in our culture. We learn to be indirect, tell little white lies, avoid the difficult topic, and so on. Being the bearer of sad tidings or bad news is not much fun. It requires great love and empathy for the person hearing such things. The difficult message also requires serious consideration about the words chosen and the amount of detail shared. The truth sometimes hurts, but it should never hurt more than is absolutely necessary, and the truth should never be told with the intention of condemning the other parent, expressing rage, or making yourself look good.

Unfortunately, parents who are going through a difficult divorce can use the truth to bash the other parent. This practice is inexcusable. It does inestimable damage to your children in the process and deepens the animosity between the adults. Divorce is a most difficult time. Anyone going through it needs understanding friends, good legal advice, supportive relatives, and whatever other adult support they can rally around them. With these trusted adults, it might be permissible to unload some rage, pain, disappointment, and even hatred.

Not so with your kids. Leave them out of the gruesome details and angry judgments, as the following quote underlines:

"My parents' divorce was ugly. I had to go and testify in the court three times. My advice for parents is to never put your kids in the middle of things. Try not to involve them in too much stuff, especially picking which parent the child has to stay with."

Your children may ask difficult, pointed questions. They may also ask in very sympathetic, understanding ways. It is okay to answer their questions in a loving, nonjudgmental way. Your children may give lots of signals that they are willing to take sides. Discourage that. Your children may seem to be handling things so well, you begin to use them as confidants. Don't! Listen to this wise advice, offered by a 15-year-old girl:

"Don't look to your kids for emotional support. I was going through so much of my own emotional hell that my mom leaning on me was the last thing that I wanted, and it made me very, very resentful of her. My mom tried to use me as her confidant for all the bad stuff my dad did to her, but she refused to see that he was still my dad, and I still loved him."

A final point of clarification: Parents should be honest about themselves and their own pain and shortcomings. Being "honest" on behalf of the other parent can all too easily constitute blame rather than honesty. The old adage "When you can't say something nice, don't say anything at all" may have great utility in sorting out these complex issues.

CALLING IN REINFORCEMENTS

Sometimes, even the best possible intentions are derailed by the way life works out, or by a variety of circumstances beyond your control. An unhappy marriage reverberates in the lives of the children, no matter what parents do. The path of least damage is that of open communication, loving honesty, parental restraint in emotions and blaming behaviors, and an absolute absence of violence or hostility. That said, however, it must be acknowledged a great deal of shock and pain arise in the coming apart of most marriages, as this 14-year-old respondent states:

"I remember the sinking feeling I got in the pit of my stomach when my parents had my brother and me sit down at the kitchen table. My mother just kept sobbing, while my father relayed in a calm manner that sometimes things in life just don't work out. My parents' divorce came as a complete shock to my brother and me. Sure, my parents had their arguments, but so did everybody from time to time. Divorce was something that happened to other people."

Talking and being open may not be possible, or it may not be enough. Adults who experienced divorce as children tell us that parents should do their best to make other, trusted people available to the children as confidants. These confidants should not take sides or pry, but just be there to help the children process their anxiety and sadness. Lois, a 60-year-old woman, remembered,

"We asked to talk with someone—doctor, priest, friend, anyone—but no, we were a proud, private, religious family and divorce was a no-no. It would bring disgrace upon our mother. Never mind what us kids needed. We even felt isolated from family friends because of the divorce. We thought it was because they pulled away from us, but later we found out that it was Mother who had pulled away in shame."

Lois reminds us that parents must not put their own pride or needs for privacy above their children's emotional health. It may be hard to seek the help the children need, but it may alleviate a great deal of pain for them, both in the present and in the future.

STAY TOGETHER FOR THE KIDS?

Even though we didn't ask directly about it, this topic was often addressed by the interview participants and people who wrote to us. What about staying in a bad relationship for the sake of the kids? Do people who have been through it look back and tell others to stay together at all costs? Lots of the people we talked to volunteered strong opinions about life before a divorce—about life with parents who do not love each other. A 16-year-old said,

"One thing, don't stay together for the kids. If the parents aren't happy, then the children will know it and possibly feel at fault."

Another stated,

"My parents have been separated and in the process of divorce for the past 5 years. The last 5 years have been very nasty between my parents and the whole family. My advice would be for parents to not stay together for the kids' sake. It does nothing but terrorize the kids."

We repeatedly heard this warning:

"It is okay to get a divorce when you are having major problems. Just don't stay together for the kid's sake. It doesn't work."

Children do not want to feel responsible for their parents' unhappiness. Furthermore, they clearly do not want to live in a home filled with anger, sadness, bitterness, silence, or abuse. They want loving, stable parents. This is well expressed by a letter to "Dear Abby," which included this statement,

"I would have much preferred that my parents had separated. They did me no favor by showing me that married life could be miserable. They were distant and cold, and that hurt me worse than a divorce ever could have."

Many individuals who responded to our survey encouraged married people to put great effort into trying to have a good marriage.

"Try really hard,"

wrote one boy.

"If the love was there once, maybe you can find it again."

But if you've tried, and you cannot find the love again, the message is clear: Don't stay together, in less than loving circumstances, for the kids' sake. They don't want it—and they don't want to live with it. Elizabeth, an 18-year-old girl who dealt for years with every hassle of joint custody, including switching houses week after week, said,

"Obviously they [her parents] should have planned it out better in the beginning and thought a little more about getting married. On the other hand, there are a lot of people that stay together and it's not a good family at all; they don't talk or have dinner together. They say they are staying together because it is morally right, or whatever, but they are not happy and that un-

happiness rubs off on the kids. So then they have this weird idea of family, and that can result in abuse and stuff. I think that sometimes, divorce is a good idea. Sure, in the beginning it is going to be hard, but in the long run the two parents are going to be happy and that will rub off on the kids. I think it would have been fine if my parents had stayed together, but if they didn't love each other they may have had affairs, and that would have been worse. And if they weren't happy, I am glad that they got a divorce. Don't stay in an unhappy relationship, that would just be a lifetime of yuck."

Another 12-year-old boy who had endured years of fighting and turmoil between his parents stated,

"I think divorce is a good thing. Sure, it breaks the family apart somewhat but if it's kind and the kids still see the parents, then it's great. Better than the fighting."

Beth, a 17-year-old girl, told us,

"To parents, I say, don't say you're staying together for the kids. If you need to get out of the relationship, do it. Don't play the blame game with each other... keep the kids out of it."

And finally, Tim, a 12-year-old boy, shared,

"All of my friends' parents, most of them aren't divorced, and I go over and wish that my house was like that. They don't fight, they don't have to move their stuff, they never have to miss anyone. At my mom's house, I miss my dad, and at my dad's house, I miss my mom. I think that my life would be a lot better if my parents got along and could still be married, but if they didn't get along, and were still married, that would be way worse."

SUMMARY

In this chapter, we addressed that awful time when things aren't going well in a marriage or committed relationship, and divorce or separation is a possibility. Children who have lived through that time had much to say. They don't want to be brought into the battles, they don't want to witness the fighting, and they don't want to take sides. They do want to be informed and protected. They don't like surprises, and they don't like being treated as if they don't exist or as if they can't see what is going on.

Some respondents were quite thankful for their parents' divorce, but for the most part, children want their parents to try to work things out. They want a loving, safe home. On the other hand, they were also clear about this: Don't stay in a bad relationship "for the kids' sake." Even though it is a difficult request, children ask their parents to be there for them in thoughtful, loving, protective ways, even if their marriage is coming apart.

CHAPTER 2

Setting Up the
Rhythm of the New Life

This chapter contains advice, comments, and stories about the process of setting up two households after parents separate. It is often a bumpy, confusing road because there are so many needs to consider, and emotions are so raw. Many state laws specify that a parenting plan be submitted at the time of divorce. A divorce may not be granted until a suitable parenting plan has been developed and agreed upon by both parties. A parenting plan must include a specific outline for how the financial and physical care of the children will be handled. Even if not required by law, a detailed plan for the children's care is an essential component of a child-friendly divorce. Check chapter 8 for resource ideas on parenting plans.

FORGET "CUSTODY"

You may notice that in this chapter, we avoid using the term *custody*. Many researchers and family experts believe that custody (as in one parent gets it and one parent does not) is a destructive and outdated concept—once a parent, always a parent. Divorce does not change one's status in terms of the obligations of parenting. A parenting plan that is designed around the needs and realities of the family coming apart is a much better concept than custody, which insinuates that somebody is granted full parenting power, while the other is relegated to being something less than a real parent. Certainly, in this world, there are bad parents, irresponsible parents, destructive par-

I would Like for my mom to come back.

ents, and negligent parents. We need to continually work to teach people better parenting behaviors. But marriage isn't necessary to become a parent, and divorce does not release parents from the parenting role and responsibilities.

PARENTAL CONTACT

Almost all children have a deep and natural longing to know and be with both of their biological parents. This can be threatening or upsetting to a parent who believes the other parent is a bad or undesirable person. One parent can feel betrayed if he or she has been more actively involved in raising the children and yet the children still want to know or spend time with the less involved parent. Parents who see themselves as having good character, good limits, and good values are sometimes divorced from people whom they believe to have bad character, bad boundaries, bad habits, or horrible values. Understandably, "good" parents can be fearful that exposure to the other parent will damage the children's development.

Even in less extreme cases, it may just be hard to let go and share the children with the other parent. Scheduling might be a hassle, or the situation may feel unfair because the other parent does not seem to try as hard, make as many sacrifices, or contribute as much to the children's needs. Whatever the case, do not take this frustration out on the kids. Their desire to stay connected with that other parent is natural. It is not meant to hurt either parent.

It may help to realize that even happy, well-adjusted, adopted children, when they reach adolescence, often feel a strong desire to seek out their biological parents or at least to obtain as much information about them as possible. This desire does not mean that the children are dissatisfied with their adoptive parents; the impulse comes from an understandable and powerful desire to become more deeply acquainted with themselves through knowing their biological parents.

Kim, an 18-year-old girl, wrote,

"What would really be good is that both parents stay in the picture. Actually, I have two fathers. My mom got remarried when I was about 9 months old and my brother was 3. My first father I truly don't know, which I think is really wrong. Even though he gave me up for my second father to adopt me, I still feel as if he made a mistake. In having two kids, he should be responsible enough to talk to us at least once a month. To make sure we truly know who we are. He is a part of me and I him, so I think that I should know some of his background, and know what my other half is like."

Most of the young people we talked with expressed a strong desire to have as close and connected relationship with each parent as possible, even if that parent wasn't the best parent in the world. Dee, a mid-life professional adult whose parents divorced while she was in her teens said,

"My dad is a total control freak. He's a jealous man, and difficult to figure out. But you know what? My mom didn't tell me any of that. She let me figure it out for myself. And she let me go ahead and love him, because he's my father—certainly not because he's perfect. I think she was overjoyed to finally get away from him, and I don't blame her, but she never ran him down or stood in the way of my time with him."

One young man told us,

"Everyone talks about 'father hunger' these days. Deadbeat dads and stuff. But mother hunger is a real thing too and is just as painful. I want to tell divorcing parents, 'Hey, make sure both parents have plenty of time with the kids.'"

As much as possible, children want both parents involved in the day-to-day aspects of their lives, as well as the big milestones, as Chad, age 10, points out:

"Both parents should try to come and see the kids' events because they can only do certain things once. The kids should love both parents, even if they get married again, and the kid could pray about the situation too."

I think A Kid Need A Mouther and A fauther. Or some wone whoe cares.

Children can be quite resilient and resourceful when they need to be. Part of what helps them be resilient is feeling secure in the knowledge that they are loved. One of the ways children feel loved and secure is to have regular contact with both of their parents. One respondent told us,

> *"Both parents need to spend time with each child separately. You need to make time for all of your kids and make sure they are doing well. Take them shopping, go to dinner, talk to them one-on-one. That is the most important thing."*

As we covered in the last chapter, another way children feel loved and respected is when parents take time to talk with them, honestly and directly. Children do not appreciate being left out, as this 11-year-old girl says:

> *"I think kids really want a family with two parents. My mom lives in another town and she goes to school and sometimes people tease me about that. I'm kind of mad at my mom for not talking to me and my little brother and my big brother. I suggest that moms and dads talk to their kids."*

RESIDENTIAL ARRANGEMENTS

This advice from a 15-year-old boy sums up a very important set of basics:

"Never put the children in the middle. Keep the children informed. Ask their opinion on things, such as housing."

Determining a sound parenting plan is challenging. Creativity, flexibility, and open communication with everyone involved is essential, because many different types of residential arrangements exist. This is true for a number of reasons, the first of which is the fact that every family is different. The relationships and needs of each individual within the family are unique, too. Families have financial and geographic realities that must be considered. The diversity of arrangements reflects the fact that the needs of any particular child or set of children cannot be met by following a cookbook approach. The ideal parenting plan should reflect what is in each child or each set of children's best interest. Because no "one size fits all" plan exists, families and those who help families during divorce are forced to do the best we can in figuring it out.

Another important point is this: Parenting plans need to change as the members of the divorced family grow and change. Although children change and grow most dramatically, all people change over time. Needs, circumstances, and relationships change. What worked beautifully for a set of toddlers and two divorced but single parents will perhaps need significant alterations to be a good arrangement for adolescents who have a remarried dad and a mom who is dating.

When talking with us, some kids, in frustration, stated that they believed the children should be allowed to decide their own residential arrangements and parenting relationships. However, as you can hear in the words of this 16-year-old girl, most children have deep ambivalence about choosing between parents:

"The custody arrangements that are best for the kids is what the kids pick, not the courts. For some children, switching from parent to parent will work. However, that will not work for others. The hardest thing I had to deal with was when my parents would fight and get me in the middle of it. By doing this, they would expect me to pick a side. I thought it was very childish and selfish of them to put me in the middle."

Although the frustration is understandable and the need to be heard is very real, the final say should not be the burden of the children. Even though allowing the children to choose seems like a great solution, it does just what the children say they do not want: It puts them in the middle. Most experts feel that children should have a great deal of input in setting up the arrangements, but ultimately should not bear the responsibility of the final decisions. Such a plan frees the children from being blamed or from blaming themselves for choosing one parent over the other. Nate was in the sixth grade when he found out that his parents were going to get divorced. He felt pressure from both parents:

> *"They were both being as nice as they possibly could to me. The way they were acting was like I could pick pretty much what I wanted. All I knew was that I was not going to choose between them. That was ridiculous."*

The turmoil and artificiality created when parents are trying to outbid each other for a child's affections are very hard on children. One 17-year-old girl remembered,

> *"My parents' divorce got worse as it went on. They started off at peace with one another, but later on they became jealous of what the other had, and they competed with each other, putting me in the middle. Don't do that! I was spoiled by both of my parents because they were trying to top each other. When they eventually stopped (or rather it slowed down, and life wasn't a constant shopping spree) it was very hard to adjust. I had a hard time."*

When parents try to gain and hold a child's affections manipulatively, children can become manipulative in return. Ultimately, this can damage the child's sense of authenticity. This angry 15-year-old girl wrote,

> *"I've turned myself inside out a million times for both of them and now I want to know which is me."*

Even if children are quite willing to choose one parent over the other at a given time, it is not necessarily wise to allow them to do so. Children live in the present and are unable to project the realistic consequences of their actions. They may make the choice for reasons that ultimately will not be in their own best interests. As Mark Twain so aptly observed many years ago, "When I was 14, my father was so ignorant I could hardly stand to have him around. When I got to be 21, I was astonished at how much he had learned in 7 years."

Madeline, a woman in her early 30s, was very thoughtful on this point. She told us that her custody arrangements did not mandate any time with her father. At the time of the divorce, she was only 3 years old and could not advocate for any time with her father. Consequently, she did not have the chance to develop a solid relationship with him. Now, she explained, she feels cheated, because she never experienced any kind of father-daughter relationship with her father or any other male.

"I wish my parents would have had a more set schedule so that they made sure that I got to see my dad on a regular basis. That might have helped us have a relationship. After I was grown, but before I had kids, my dad and I had such different interests that we couldn't relate, so I just ignored him and pushed him away. Now he is really into my kids, and we have them as a common ground. But for him and me, there is no special father-daughter relationship. I find myself feeling jealous and curious about that kind of bond, even watching my husband and daughter. I just look at them when they are together and say, 'What is this? What is this all about?'"

Many children who commented on this issue were wise enough to realize they really would not want the final say. Being consulted is certainly important to them, but they dreaded the scenario wherein the parents might each look imploringly at the child and say, "You choose." Asking children to choose between parents is a cop-out. Children who love both parents do not want to be asked to choose one over the other. They do want a say, however, in what happens to them and how their lives are arranged. As one 15-year-old girl pointed out,

"If children are old enough, make sure they are informed about what is going on and make sure they are involved in the decision of where they are going to live and that it's not just a cus-

*tody battle and big power struggle between the parents with
each one just trying to come out with more."*

Children often have very clear preferences in their residential
arrangements, and these preferences should be given significant
weight in the decision-making process. The parents or professionals
involved in the final decision need to able to say, "We have considered, as best we can, all the information and opinions available. Your
wishes were central to this decision, and we respect you and want
the best for you." Then when the decision is enacted, it is the
adult(s), not the child, who bears the onus of the choice.

One child, a sixth-grade boy, reported feeling torn about sharing
his thoughts with anyone. His parents were locked in bitter battle
over his residential arrangements, and he loved both of them equally.

*"I am glad there is a judge involved in this. The judge is the one
who decides. Not me. I can't say what would be best. I know my
dad really wants me to be with him and I know my mom really
wants me too. I'm happy in either place."*

Unless circumstances simply will not allow it, most respondents
felt that roughly equal time with each parent was the best situation if
parents live reasonably close to each other. One interview participant told us,

*"I think that splitting custody is the best; it is a pain moving all
your stuff, but it is worth it. There are things that I don't like
about both my parents but moving gives me sort of a break.
And I get to deal with just one of them at a time."*

Many pointed out that going back and forth is an enormous hassle
and advocated that time between switching to the other parents'
house be increased as the children get older, meaning less moving
back and forth. A few mentioned the idea of staying in the family
home themselves and having the parents come and go. Or simply
staying in one home but having lots of contact with the other parent
through vacations, outings, meals, and occasional visits. One 16-year-
old boy told us the following:

*"My mom had to move to another town, not far away, for work.
I refused to live with my dad and his girlfriend. They didn't have
room anyway. And I didn't want to switch high schools. My soc-*

cer team is the best, and they needed me. So my mom let me use the child support money and we rented this little apartment, and on weekends, she comes into town and stays with me. Dad checks in some, but he's pretty much in his own world. I have to keep my grades up and stuff, but I like it. It works for us."

The issue of choice will probably be an ongoing one for many divorced families. We address this a bit more in the next chapter. As this 15-year-old boy states,

"Let your children live with whoever they want to. Don't make them live with both parents if it is way too hard. Like if you can't go to your friend's because you're at your dad's. I like to live with my mom more than my dad, but I have to go to my mom's Monday and Wednesday and every other weekend and to my dad's Tuesday and Thursday and every other weekend. Let your kid talk to you about where they want to go and don't make them feel bad. You messed up, we didn't. But we have to pay."

Respondents often noted a big difference between the issue of where to live and the issue of parental contact. As illustrated in the next quote, most wanted lots of peaceful parental contact, and wanted to live as simply as possible:

"Keep close contact with the kids. Let them know you love them, and don't abandon them. Let the kids chose to live in a comfortable environment. Don't put pressure on them. Try to get along with your ex. It makes a big difference."

In the February 15, 1999, issue of *Newsweek* featured Nick Sheff, a 16-year-old boy, in the "My Turn" column. His essay was titled "My Long-Distance Life," and we have included excerpts here. It is a wonderfully expressive essay that captures the essence of many shorter essays we received.

"When I was 4, my parents decided that they could no longer live together. That same year, my mom moved to Los Angeles, and a therapist was hired to decide where I would live. . . . The therapist finally decided I'd stay with my dad during the school year and visit my mom on long holidays and for the summers. I began flying between two cities and two

different lives. I've probably earned enough miles for a round-trip ticket to Mars. Some people love to fly, but I dreaded the trips . . .

I remember the last day of school in sixth grade. All my friends made plans to go to the beach together—all my friends, but not me. I had to fly to L.A. It wasn't that I didn't want to see my mom and stepdad. I just didn't want to leave my friends. As the school year came to a close, I began to shut down. I hated saying goodbye for the summer. It was easier to put up a wall, to pretend I didn't care. . . .

I am 16 now and I still travel back and forth, but it's mostly up to me to decide when. I've chosen to spend more time with my friends at the expense of visits with my mom. When I do go to L.A., it's like my stepdad put it: I have a cameo role in their lives. I say my lines and I'm off. It's painful.

What's the toll of this arrangement? I'm always missing somebody. . . . Many of my friends' parents are divorced. The ones whose mom and dad live near each other get to see both their parents more. These kids can go to school plays and dances on the weekends, and see their friends when they want.

No child should be subjected to the hardship of long-distance joint custody. To prevent it, maybe there should be an addition to the marriage vows: Do you promise, in sickness and in health, as long as you both shall live? And if you ever have children and wind up divorced, do you promise to stay within the same geographical area as your kids? Actually, since people often break those vows, maybe it should be a law: If you have children, you must stay near them. Or how about some common sense? If you move away from your children, you have to do the traveling to see them. . . . Before I have children of my own, I'll use my experiences to help make good decisions about whom I choose to marry. However, if I do get a divorce, I will put my children's needs first. I will stay near them no matter what happens."

This articulate young man captured the essence of many respondent's sentiments. Having children and raising them well is a lifelong commitment that requires significant sacrifice. Most parents have no intention of hurting their children in a divorce process, but many fail to realize that meeting the children's needs will take planning, commitment, and sacrifice.

CALMING THE STORM

Divorcing parents should keep in mind that most children do not welcome change in their physical surroundings. Initially, there will be resistance and complaints no matter how carefully the children's needs were considered. Disrupted lifestyles and habits are hard to cope with under the best of circumstances. In the midst of a divorce, with all the emotional work that needs to be done, these physical changes are made doubly hard. As one child, who had experienced separation but whose parents had subsequently moved back together, said,

"As the custody arrangements go, I don't know. No custody arrangements are good. My little sister and I were supposed to go back and forth between houses all the time, and I despised it. I almost wished I could just stay at a friend's house so I wouldn't have to keep switching."

This young person is acutely aware of the trade-offs involved when your parents are no longer living together. Moving back and forth is a hassle. But the pay-off is sharing in the day-to-day lives of both parents.

It is nearly guaranteed that initially, everyone will struggle with the new life arrangements, no matter what they are. A 12-year-old respondent offered this sage advise:

"Parents should just try to act like adults—not like fighting children. Everyone needs to have compassion and keep in mind it's not going to be an easy trip."

And we heard this succinct comment from a young man:

"Getting set up after a divorce is a pain. Don't make it any worse than it is. Forgive and forget, don't hold grudges."

Practical ideas were offered to help ease the transitions children go through in shared residential parenting. One young woman who is both a child of divorce and a professional who now works with divorcing families sent us the following list:

1. *Read divorce books to your children so they know other people go through this.*
2. *Take the kids to the store and get a nice travel bag for their trips back and forth.*
3. *Buy two sets of basic toiletries and things children need to have readily available.*
4. *Give each child something special of yours to carry with them—an old watch, a piece of jewelry, an old t-shirt, or a stuffed animal. Or make a tape of your voice reading something, or a videotape. Give them a picture of yourself, or hand write them a note. Find something that will remind them of you when you can't be with them.*
5. *Get or keep your children involved in expressive group activities such as sports, dance, art, or music. They will need ways to let out some of their pent-up emotions.*
6. *Remember, the children's needs come first. You will have new needs. Don't expect your children to meet them. Your children will have new needs. It is your job to meet them.*

One positive consequence that naturally arises out of shared parenting and time split between two parents is the potential increase in one-on-one time children get with each parent. Often, when the time you are going to get to spend with your children is limited, structured, and designated as "time with the kids," you can be more attentive and better plan your use of the time. Obviously, there will also be time when you will not be able to be with the children. One 7-year-old girl told us,

"My dad lives right here in town but I only get to see him 4 days a month."

This young girl values the time with her father very highly and wants to have more of it. It seems likely her father is making good use of the time he does have with her, even if it is limited. She looks forward to time with him, and wants more connection.

A WORD OF CAUTION

Of course, the assumption that maximal exposure to each parent is the best arrangement makes one important assumption: that each parent meets the minimum requirements for adequate parenting. In situations in which one parent has been abusive or is addicted to destructive behaviors or drugs or has character flaws of such magnitude that he or she simply cannot parent at even minimum standards, then adjustments must be made accordingly. Divorcing parents facing this situation most often need to seek professional help in determining if, when, and under what circumstances a dysfunctional parent should see the children. The truth is, kids often still want and need contact with less-than-functional parents. But they also need to be protected. The contact may need to be supervised or managed in some way so that children are not subject to manipulations by the dysfunctional parent or exposed to dangerous or damaging behaviors. For a more complete discussion of this topic, see chapter 7.

DECOUPLING MONEY FROM RELATIONSHIP

Families going through divorce have a lot of financial adjusting to do, and it will affect the children. Most children seem less concerned about money *per se* and more concerned about the effects the reduced income has on their parents and on their parents' attitudes toward each other. This young woman was 11 years old when her parents divorced:

"When I first learned about their plans to separate, I was more shocked than devastated. The most difficult part of the entire divorce for me was seeing what my mother had to go through. She was always stressed and upset, frequently crying. The financial situation was terrible, and the conversations between my mother and my father were truly heart breaking. It hurt me so much to see how my mother suffered."

As we have discussed, children want to be told the truth, but it is the parents' job to frame the truth in developmentally sensitive ways. The truth about the financial failings of one parent should never be used to frighten children or play on their sympathies. And the truth

Think about your kids! Listen to your kids! Make sure you always remember that they are a human being! Not just something that is juggled around. And make sure you let them do what they what to do. Because you have to realize that your time (as they call it) is actually there time.

should not be told in such a way as to make the child into the "man" or "woman" of the house. As this wise 16-year-old advised,

"Don't allow the oldest child to become parentified. Putting them in charge of younger siblings, finances, and meals may seem like a viable option during such a chaotic time. However, the oldest child can be stripped of his or her childhood."

Naturally, children object to being treated as "part of the divorce settlement." As this 10-year-old girl urged,

"Think about your kids! Listen to your kids! Make sure you always remember that they are a human being, not just something that is juggled around. And make sure you let them do what they want to do because you have to realize that 'your time' (as they call it) is actually their time."

Payment of child support is a particularly emotion-laden component of divorce. It is easy to see how it becomes entangled with parental contact, because the children's financial needs will travel with them to some extent. Whoever has the children more often faces higher grocery bills, phone bills, utility bills, fuel bills, and so on. Although the ideal is establishing large enough homes so that the children have their own space in each parents' home, it may not be economically feasible. A good parenting plan needs to take all of this into account. Both parents are responsible for the care of their children, which costs money. It takes time, energy, and resources. Adults who are separating from each other must determine how each aspect of their children's needs will be met. This should be done as fairly as possible, and should be done as a separate issue from property settlement, maintenance payments, and other aspects of the coming-apart process.

One 19-year-old woman told us proudly,

"My parents never exchanged a dime of child support. I spent pretty much equal time at both places. They told me that they decided, when they divorced, that each of them wanted me so much they thought of having me with them as a privilege, not something the other one should pay them for. I was only six at the time, but I've come to appreciate that."

Many of our respondents reported feeling especially angry when their contact with one parent was limited because that parent was not making child support payments. In the case of children and divorce, money for time is a bad idea. Dave, a respondent in his 30s, told us this story:

"We lived primarily with my mother, who remarried. We had a nice house and stuff. My dad really struggled though. He was supposed to pay child support every month, but the business he ran didn't do very well, and sometimes he got behind. I could tell because he wouldn't come to see us as much. Then the business went bankrupt, and he couldn't pay child support at all. I could tell he felt terrible. He didn't come around much at all. When we saw him, he started to discuss money as the reason he couldn't come around much. That wasn't normal for him. I knew how much it hurt for my dad to have to turn his back on my sister and me."

Financial arrangements, residential arrangements, and parenting plans should not be approached as win-lose situations. The process should involve striving for the best possible arrangements—with the children's needs coming first. The children and their needs should not be among the divorce bargaining chips. Fathers and mothers should not see themselves as "paying up" so they can have contact with their children. Of course, both parents should pay their fair share of the costs associated with the children's financial needs, and they should put in the time and energy necessary to meet the children's emotional needs. But quite simply, these two obligations should not be tangled up together. Finances and relationship are essential, but separate, parental duties. As this 18-year-old boy said,

"You don't want to get your children caught up in the money situation. Parents need to be responsible to help with money for their kids in any way they can. They need to be there for their kids. But the most important thing isn't money. Think about your kids."

SPLITTING SIBLINGS?

Sometimes, divorcing families consider separating the siblings from one another in the new parenting arrangements. Some of our respondents had strong (and varied) feelings about this concept. One woman who was a child of divorced parents shared,

"My mother intended to split my brother and me up to be raised by different people, but my dad intervened. I am glad that the split never happened, and so is my brother. Having already experienced so much turmoil, I do not think we could have handled being separated. We anchored each other during the storm, and I would certainly urge divorcing parents not to divide children between them."

The same sentiment is echoed in the following account, also given by a woman in her 50s:

"To this day, we all remember the station wagon pulling away with Doris and me in it, and our brother chasing it, yelling and sobbing, 'Bring back my sisters. Don't take them away!' We watched through the rear window and cried and screamed for our brother."

In the latter case, the siblings were reunited after a year apart, but not without a great deal of family conflict and hardship.

We also spoke with siblings who found it a great relief to live apart. Ryan, a 12-year-old boy, said quite clearly,

"I cannot get along with my sister. She is impossible. I know I don't hate her completely, but if I had to live with her at Dad's, I think I would kill myself."

In this family, the best of all possible worlds seemed to be having the siblings live separately with different parents. There were planned times in the schedule for the siblings to have meals together at each parents' house, but everyone agreed it was better to have each living primarily with one parent and spending far less time at the other parents' house. Leah, who was 5 years old when her parents divorced, remembers living with each parent off and on. Even after the divorce, her parents fought continually, with Leah taking her father's side and Leah's sister taking her mother's side. She told us,

"My sister lives with my mom now, and I live with my dad, and it is much more peaceful. I still see my sister and we get along okay, but this is better. It just worked out better this way."

Terry, a 19-year-old young man, said,

"I don't have much to complain about in my parents' divorce. It was when I was in second grade and I don't remember a lot of it too clearly. My dad moved and took my older brother with him. It was just like, my brother wanted to go with him and I didn't. So that's what they did. I visited them for most of the summer, and it was a little strange. When my dad remarried, I felt sorry for my brother. Our stepmom is a bitch. I would say to divorcing families, 'Do what makes you happy.' There isn't a perfect way, but life's not perfect."

Again, finances, logistics, individual needs, and relationships all must be carefully considered when choices about residential arrangements are made. What is best for one family may be a tragedy for another.

PARENTING ACROSS THE MILES

This 18-year-old boy was clear in the advice he offered:

"To fathers, I would like to say that no matter what happens, never lose contact with your child. You don't know what birthday cards, Christmas cards, or just letters actually mean to your

children. In my parents' divorce, my dad took off and I never got anything from him. Even though you get through it and move on, the question 'Why doesn't he want me?' always remains."

Divorcing people may feel they would like to live as far from their ex-spouses as possible. When no children are involved, this seems logical and fine. However, children develop and maintain more healthy attachments to their parents by being able to see each one on a consistent, predictable and frequent basis. Carol, looking back on her time with her father, said,

"I wish that I knew more of the little things about my dad's daily routines. I missed out on any sort of rituals or traditions with my dad because I just didn't see him often enough. I was glad when I could go see him, but that was less than once a year."

It may not be possible for divorcing parents to set up households in the same neighborhood, but it is worth trying to stay as close and available as possible.

A boy whose parents divorced when he was 13 years old reported that he had only spoken with his mother once in the last 5 years and offered this advice:

"I think the best advice would be to live in kind of the same area; not a thousand miles from each other."

Another child's comment was succinct and revealing:

"Don't move away and forget you have kids."

And another, a high school sophomore, noted gratefully,

"On the subject of custody I think my parents handled it pretty well. They try to make no inconvenience for the kids, and that's nice. I think I would like to stay with each parent longer because then moving back and forth isn't such a hassle. I think it's also good that my parents live near each other, only five blocks apart."

Although proximity makes co-parenting much more realistic, after a divorce, parents often do move away at some point. Craig, a 12-year-old boy whose mother decided to move to a town 3 hours away to live with her boyfriend, said,

"If I could tell my mom the truth, I would tell her that when she decided to move I felt like she didn't like me anymore, because she was just leaving. I would tell moms to tell their kids that they don't not like them anymore, that they still want to be with their kids."

Remember, a divorce provides freedom from being with someone you can no longer love or with whom you can no longer share a home. It should not provide freedom from your parenting responsibilities or from serious consideration of the effects your actions will have on your children. If it is absolutely necessary to move away from your children, explaining this to them multiple times is essential so that they understand the real reasons you are leaving them. Do not leave them to speculate.

Even if some of it comes from a distance, consistent, regular, and frequent contact matters to your children and to their healthy development. One child said,

"Talk to your children about divorce and what it means. Please tell them that it doesn't mean that you both don't love them anymore. Keep in touch with your children. Try to be there for them, even if you're far away."

That last sentence is a statement of hope. Divorced parents can be there for their kids, even if they are not able to be physically present. Pictures, videotapes, letters, phone calls, packages, even faxes and e-mails are all relatively simple ways to let children know they are loved on a daily basis from anywhere on the globe.

In cases of great distance, the residential parent can play an important role in keeping the distant relationship alive. One of our adult respondents told us, with gratitude and admiration for her father,

"Even though my father had custody of us, he made sure we wrote to my mom and visited her. There was never an attitude that we were exclusively his."

This is a wonderful example of a father who was proactive in helping his children maintain a relationship with their mother.

WHEN IT'S DOWN TO ONE

When children are living predominantly or exclusively with one parent, it is not unusual for them to develop fears about losing that parent. An 8-year-old girl told us,

> *"I feel really afraid sometimes that my mom will leave me. She has custody mostly. What if she needed to leave the state like my dad did?"*

And a woman in her 40s wrote,

> *"My brother and I lived with my dad and sometimes I would worry that he might die. I would sit in school, but I couldn't pay attention sometimes because I would think about what might happen in the future."*

We interviewed a few children of divorce who were quite young. They often did not quite understand the concept of offering advice to adults, but they still had important insights into their own worlds and needs. Six-year-old Willy, whose father had left the state and had not maintained contact for several years, told us,

> *"I'm glad I have a mom. I love my mommy. I'm six and a half and I know how to read good."*

Willy and the other children quoted in this section help us glimpse how vital a child's connection to a single parent may be. These children need extra reassurance of their parents' love and stability. One parent has already completely or mostly disappeared. This experience brings an awareness that contact with a parent can be lost, and a fear that it will happen again. We return to this topic in more depth in chapter 7.

LIFE IN TWO LANES (CO-PARENTED CHILDREN)

> *"I think that each parent should have the same rules as the other."*

This statement by an 11-year-old girl articulates a problem associated with many uncomfortable co-parenting conflicts. A 17-year-old boy offered simple guidelines that just might help:

"Don't hold grudges. Don't treat your children as possessions. Share time together. Be nice to one another. Try and remain friends for the kids' sake."

Divorce does not mean parents should stop parenting *together*. Most children can adjust to minor parenting differences, but consistency between households is an important element of family life when there are two separate families involved. Kids need and want to know the family expectations and rules. And if the rules are broken, fair and predictable consequences are an important part of healthy child-rearing. Parents are sometimes tempted to loosen up on the rules, hoping to gain a favored status in the eyes of the children. Similarly, parents are often guilty of getting into one-upmanship battles with regard to such things as gifts, later curfews, or reduced household chores to try and be seen as the "cooler" or more valued parent.

Parenting meetings and check-ins are often a great (and difficult) idea when divorced people are co-parenting. Decisions about child-rearing practices such as bedtime, diet, religious education, medications, dental care, homework, TV viewing, exercise, music lessons, sports, and art activities require the input and informed support of both parents. Some kids reported that their parents (and stepparents) would phone or get together every so often to update calendars, talk over child-related matters, and make joint decisions.

Interparent communication is essential to a stable life for a child living in two households, but pitfalls must be avoided as parents struggle to keep those tense lines of communication open. Together, they have to try and sort out what plan they think is best for their kids. Should she have a car? Should he work in the summer? What kind of chores should be expected or allowances given? Though they may not enjoy it, effective divorced parents are a team.

Married couples do not always have identical opinions, but they are viewed by children as a united force; this allows kids to freely speak their mind or even side with one parent without worrying that they are insulting, hurting, or even abandoning the other. Kids of divorce can be afraid to say what they want if what they want happens to align with only one parent's opinion. Because they are no longer dealing with a loving couple, they end up having to choose to step on one side or the other of a defined and tense parental boundary.

Karen, an 18-year-old girl, described the crux of the divorced child's loyalty dilemma:

"I wish my parents were less stubborn, that they would sometimes just give a little. I can never do anything that pleases them both. I am always disappointing someone."

Divorced parents must realize that a decision made "in favor" of one parent is not a decision based in any way on the amount of love the child has for that parent. There is no need to feel as if decisions in a child's life are a battle that can be lost or won. These decisions are just forks in the road; sometimes things will go the direction you see as best and sometimes not.

Divorced parents must be cautious of decision-making patterns. Liz, age 13, shared the following frustration:

"Lots of times there are decisions to be made, and my parents get so caught up in their opinions, they make decisions that involve me and I feel like I am not even there."

Similarly, Ethan, now 19, told us,

"My parents were divorced when I was five. They were good at having meetings and making pretty peaceful decisions on things such as what summer camps I should go to. At first I was too young to make those decisions for myself. As I got older, they still met, and often still made decisions largely without me. When I was younger, I was glad I wasn't forced to decide anything and cause anyone to feel ganged up on or sad. What my parents didn't do as well was to integrate me into the decision-making process. I think that would have helped me understand that they were adults who did not need my protection. To this day I have trouble simply deciding what I want if there is a conflict between my parents. Even last year, I spent Christmas and Thanksgiving frantically trying to eat meals with everyone who invited me. This even included grandparents!"

Well-loved children sometimes develop great sensitivity toward the needs of their loved ones. Helping them find themselves in the midst of all that love and its implied obligations can be an important and advanced parenting task for co-parenting parents. The

drawing above is by a 6-year-old girl. There are many things the picture might reveal, but the most obvious is this: Here are two children who have a distinct family life with Mom and a distinct family life with Dad. Although this may be the very best solution in the case of divorcing parents, we should always remember it is a complicated and demanding life for the children.

SUMMARY

In this chapter, we covered advice and ideas about how to maximize contact with each parent without unduly stressing the children. Sorting out the competing needs and finding the best parenting patterns is hard work and must be revisited as families change and children's developmental needs change. Children do not want to be asked to choose between their parents, and they do not want child support payments to be linked directly to their time with a certain parent. As they grow and develop, they want an increasingly strong voice in their living arrangements, but they also want loving guidance and structure from their parents.

When parents choose or are forced to move away, it adds even greater stress and difficulty for the children. Even so, there are ways parents at a distance can bridge the gap and stay involved in their children's lives.

Finally, whether far away or close by, children need parents who communicate with each other and who attempt to create consistent, supportive home environments. They resent being treated as a commodity with rigid time schedules for contact with each parent and little flexibility for the natural ebb and flow of life.

CHAPTER 3

Dealing With
the Other Parent

When people define the term *divorce*, they usually speak of the end of a relationship between two people. Divorce means the marriage is over, the vows are nullified, and the two adults involved begin separate lives. When children are involved, divorce is the ending of one form of relationship between the parents—and the beginning of another. For the mother of the children, divorce changes her *husband* into the *father of her children*. For the father, divorce changes his *wife* into the *mother of his children*. They become co-parents, and to be effective co-parents, a certain level of civility in the relationship is required. Co-parenting, at least according to many divorced parents, is not exactly enjoyable most the time. In fact, most consider it to be a real drag. And according to the children of divorce, many parents aren't pulling it off that well.

FOR THE KIDS' SAKE, GET ALONG

The heading of this section is probably the most important thing we will share in this entire book—and the hardest assignment a divorced parent can be given. After all, if the two parents in question found it easy, or even possible, to get along, they probably wouldn't have gotten divorced. Nevertheless, it is the plea echoed in almost every interview, every essay, every chat, and every counseling session we have ever had with children of divorce. The following cluster of quotes capture this ever-present request. They also reflect the often-expressed frustration children feel toward their divorced parents. It is a tedious, redundant list for most people to read. To make it sink in, try to imagine a whole room full of all ages of kids, all sizes, colors, and shapes. Imagine curly hair, straight hair, short skirts, baggy pants, big grins, serious looks, imploring eyes, and voices in a chorus, saying the various quotes that follow:

"Parents need to realize that when they divorce each other they don't divorce their child."

"All I have to say is that when parents get divorced it really sucks when they badmouth each other in front of the kids."

"Try to get along for the kid's sake."

"Do not fight or argue in front of kids and do not bring kids into your fights! Do not have them pick sides and do not talk badly about the other one in front of the kids because it just hurts more!"

"Around children in the family you shouldn't argue or fight or talk about your problems. You should remain friends to cause less havoc in the child's life."

"The best advice I can give is never say anything bad about your ex-spouse. It only makes your child feel bad about caring for your ex."

"I think parents need to know that they shouldn't put their kids in the middle. One parent shouldn't tell their kids how bad the other is or how much they hate the other one, or use their kids as a go-between."

"I was put in the middle as referee, carrier pigeon, and counselor. The only advice I want to offer is don't be so childish. Leave the kids out of it. And get feelings resolved and get closure."

"The best thing is to make sure the parents have a courteous relationship and do not belittle or degrade each other in front of others. I am not saying you have to stay best friends, just try to keep a friendly, open line of communication."

"Don't bad mouth the other parent."

"Don't feed your kids full of propaganda, and don't blame all of the negative things about your kids on the other parent to the children's face."

"Never, never involve the kids in your fights. Do not talk about the other parent negatively to the child or try to get to each other through the children. Just think about the kids even when it comes to the adult's own sacrifice and pain."

"Sometimes my parents talk about each other, but I have trained myself to just stare at something and tune them out."

To round out this adamant list, the box on this page contains a series of points written by a young woman who described her parents' divorce as mean, nasty, ugly, awful, immature, hostile, stupid, petty, and ridiculous.

---

1. Never, never, never say *anything* other than kind things about your ex. You know that old saying, "If you can't say anything nice don't say anything at all"? It wasn't just for your 3-year-old.

2. Either (a) buy your kids two of everything, or (b) have them live with one parent and visit the other, or (c) have the switching-house ritual as seldom as possible. Living your life out of a suitcase is an enormous drag. For most of my life, I've spent more time at summer camps than I ever did at one house.

3. Your children are your children. They are not negotiators, mediators, or go-betweens of any kind. If you have something to say to your ex, say it to your ex, not to your kid.

4. Don't let the kids play you off each other. If your child is mad at you, let her call your ex and complain, but the two of you should have an agreement: No fostering negative feelings on the phone, no untimely switch of locale, whoever has custody at the moment makes the rules—all the rules—and is in charge of enforcing them.

5. You loved each other enough to bring children into the world. Try to act like adults when conflicts arise. Kids don't like acting in the parental role.

6. It's not "your time" or "his time." It's the child's *life*.

Study after study about children's adjustment to divorce admonish parents to bite their tongues when it come to talking negatively about the other parent. But negative, contentious behavior and talk-between their parents was the number one complaint of the young people with whom we talked. To request that people be civil and even kind to someone who has hurt, disappointed, and betrayed them is a large request and requires admirable levels of self-restraint and maturity, but it is a gift of great love to your children. Perhaps even more difficult is the act of encouraging children to love and spend time with the other parent rather than always vying for the child's favor and time selfishly.

KINDNESS AS DAMAGE CONTROL

You may read the heading of this section and think, "Oh, of course, I am very kind to my children." But that's not who we are talking about. Ironically, kindness toward your ex-spouse is a form of damage control for your kids. One respondent told us,

"Even while I was a child, and certainly now as an adult, I am extremely grateful for the fact that my parents never spoke disparagingly of each other in my presence. Their conflicts were not necessarily hidden from me, but I was not treated as a confidant or sounding board. Because of this, I was left with the impression that whatever had transpired between them, they were never sorry that my brother and I had been born. It was not a matter of being told this (words are very cheap things). Had they merely verbalized that they cared for me, but then used me to air their grievances about each other, I would have felt that perhaps I was not really wanted and that I was a mistake from their past and that I reminded them of this other person that they disliked and were trying to rid themselves of. But by exhibiting a modest respect for each other and talking to me, they demonstrated to me as a child that they respected what they had created together."

Dysfunctional families, bad marriage relationships, and divorces are hard on children. As our teenage friends and respondents would say, "Duh." But the challenges and damages can be minimized or made much worse, depending on the behavior of the adults involved. When interviewed, not many young people indicated that they felt harmed *simply* by the divorce of their parents. In fact, quite

Don't blame eachother Say Yes
I did this and it was wrong. Then
the other person should say
the same thing.

a few mentioned at least a few positive outcomes, and a few were even glad their parents got divorced. Still, fighting, slander, bitterness, and failure to move on were often cited as severely damaging. As one young adolescent put it,

> *"Dysfunctional families suck. Open up your eyes and look at what is happening to most kids in the world today. The kid will always think that it is his or her fault, which leads to an unhappy, mentally hurt, and troublesome life. My suggestion is don't get married and especially, don't have children if you can't get along."*

Many adult children of divorce blame what they believe to be flaws in their character on their parents' bickering and backstabbing. Kevin, a man in his early 30s who told us he had recently joined a men's group, reported,

> *"My parents were awful about relating to each other. Basically, my mom treated my dad like scum. And he wasn't that bad of a guy. He didn't pay what he was supposed to for child support, and it made her crazy. I wanted to see him, but she made me feel bad. You know, the way I got stuck in the middle created anger in me that only recently, like in the last month, have I started to figure out. I snap very easily, I have very little patience, and boy, for some reason I just lash out."*

Tonya, in her late teens, shared,

> *"If Dad just could have avoided telling me that first bitter story about money, things would have been a lot better."*

Her father felt ripped off by her mother in the divorce settlement and could not stop himself from telling Tonya how terrible he felt and how much he distrusted her "money-hungry" mother. Although in reality, Tonya's father may have lost some money, he vastly compounded his loss by losing some of his daughter's love and respect.

One grown child of divorced parents had this advice:

"Don't bad-mouth the other parent in front of the children. While this seems like common sense, it happens frequently! This makes it difficult for the child (even as an adult) to have a parent-child relationship with the parent that has been bad-mouthed. I know things about my father that are clearly outside the boundaries of a healthy parent-child relationship."

Exposing children to the content of adult conflicts causes damage at many levels. The fact is, children don't want to know disappointing, disgusting, or embarrassing adult information about their parents. And they certainly don't want to be exposed to constant bickering and back-stabbing. Wally, a man in his 50s, claimed,

"If it hadn't been for my parents immature fighting I think that now I would be a much softer person. Less quick to just close my heart when there is conflict."

Susan, a graduate student, stated the following,

"I believe the most damaging thing I experienced as a child of divorced parents is the anger my mom had toward my father. Justified or not, it doesn't matter. Her negative comments toward him, her refusal to do things because of him, and her rage over the pain he caused her were poured into my brothers and me. Consequently, we lived in fear of making mom mad, and we were unjustly put in the middle of the their issues. In addition, her anger toward my father colored my view of men. . . and I have since had to relearn that not all men will leave you or be unfaithful. In fact, most men are kind and loving, and it's okay to depend on them in a healthy manner. Thankfully, my father did not reciprocate her anger, although he had reason to feel the same. His constant, calm, rational approach to dealing with my mom probably prevented many years of psychotherapy."

Susan's story is especially important to remember. It is apparent that both parents hurt and disappointed each other. Both parents made mistakes. Perhaps her father's behavior was even worse than her mother's. The more important factor is that her father was calm, loving, and forgiving. Parents who insist that their ex-spouse is scum—even if they are justified in that assessment—come off as the less mature, less loving, less healthy parent. If that other parent *is* despicable, the children will figure it out on their own.

It is true that constant berating of the other parent can color children's feelings about that parent. One teenager told us,

"My mom just couldn't stop ragging about my dad. Her dishing to me about him just made it so much harder to reconstruct a relationship with him (it took 5 years before I even spoke to him again). Mom even told me that I was her 'prize' in the divorce and that my dad had gotten everything else but me. I still have a hard time with relationships and concepts like being with someone forever."

As this quote illustrates, parents have a great deal of power and can turn children against parents, at least in the short run. But this quote, and many others, make it clear: There is no doubt that such ranting is quite damaging to the children.

Forgiveness, tolerance, and even neutrality are difficult attitudes to strive for, but such qualities will give your children a much healthier, happier future. As Alex, a 16-year-old boy wrote,

"Remember, you ex is still a parent to your children. Allow your children to develop their own opinions about him or her. Children are put in a terrible position when one parent berates another. A sense of confusion about divided loyalties will occur, and children may carry guilt because of the love they feel for the parent you are bashing. Allow your children to develop their own relationships with the other parent."

THE SPIRIT OF THE LAW VERSUS THE LETTER OF THE LAW

After legal issues and living arrangements are settled and a routine is established, many kids complained that their parents became inflexible and possessive of their time with the kids. Although this attitude can send the positive message that the parent values time with their children, it can also be perceived as placing the child in an uncomfortable position. Eva, a 17-year-old-high school senior, said,

"I wish my dad was less controlling so I could stay with him, and then just go out with my mom whenever I want. My dad wants to know a week ahead of time if there are changes to the routine. That's not realistic. I mean, he doesn't even know what he'll be doing in a week."

Eva is right. Very few people, especially teenagers, can plan their social lives far in advance. Parental rigidity can become an unfair burden for young people.

Tommy, an 8-year-old boy whose parents had been fighting, in court, over their time with him since he was 2, said,

"I like my mom okay but she doesn't understand about T-ball. I help my [step]brother, Adam, quite a bit. And my dad goes out of town, too. She gets so mad if I want to see him when it is her week. It makes me wish I just lived with my dad and visited my mom sometimes. But she doesn't have any other kids, so then I guess I should stay with her. I would tell parents to have a lot of other things to do."

Listen to Tommy's words. He is a boy stuck with divided loyalties. What makes his situation even more sad is that his parents live only a mile apart. He could easily see each of them almost every day, but each guards their time with Tommy jealously, taking one another back to court for things such as refusal to allow extra time to attend a family wedding.

A 14-year-old girl whose parents had been divorced for 12 years wrote,

"Parents (mine anyway) are really stupid and immature. They can't communicate, or even pretend to get along. When two people make the choice to have and raise a child, they should make a full commitment—no slacking. If they do have to get divorced, they should stay committed to a good upbringing for the child, regardless of how much they hate each other. No selfishness: tax deductions, child support, or whatever. If you love your kids enough—you would choose what's best for them, because that is what they deserve."

This child wasn't asking for parents who acted like best friends. She simply wanted them to pretend, at a distance, to get along. But even that was asking too much. Another girl echoed this plea,

"Try to be as friendly as possible in front of the kids. Even if its not totally heartfelt. Never show your anger or hate toward the other spouse in front of the kids."

And a third said,

"Try to keep civil contact with each other for the child's sake. Don't make the child feel torn or stuck in the middle."

Note the modest quality of these requests. Is civility too much to ask?

BIG EVENTS: HOW TO RUIN OR SAVE THEM

In the short, fast-paced time called childhood, most major events happen only once. School budgets are too strapped to offer an extra band concert so divorced parents can have the option of not being in the same auditorium with each other. Soccer games, spelling bees, parent-teacher conferences, choir festivals, chess matches, talent shows, even weddings—you name it, we've heard stories about parents who have spoiled it. Stop for a minute and remember your own childhood. Those of you fortunate enough to have a memory of a parent who came to important events, remember one of those. Now imagine the parent refusing to come because the other parent might be there, or might bring a date. Imagine the stress you feel about the event, tripled because of the stress you would feel knowing one parent might fight with the other or treat the other poorly. Imagine the stress of being in the middle. You might even get blamed. After all, you were the one with the event.

Children want and need parental support for their efforts, and they will remember that support fondly for the rest of their lives. They will also remember—with bitterness—the times their events and special moments became nightmares because of their parents' animosities.

Karen's father, 16 years after the divorce, is still so mad at her mother that he can barely greet her in public.

"At my graduation, my mom saved a seat for my dad, but he wouldn't sit by her. So my sister got so mad she sat by herself because she told them that she was not going to choose between them. I still see all of my extended family and parents, so it doesn't feel at all like my family is torn apart except when my

dad does dumb stuff like that. I always worried about things like concerts at school, and if they would sit by each other and if they would be civil. They ruined a lot of good things."

Shawna, a college freshman, remembers,

"My mom never saw me touch a basketball. I played for 6 years straight. Our team went to state twice. My dad was a fanatic and a great athlete. My mom couldn't stand the fact that he left her for his secretary. But I paid the price, too. I didn't leave her. But in a way, she left me. She would never be anywhere he was going to be."

And Amy, a fourth grader, reported,

"It's embarrassing that my teacher has to meet at different times with my mom and my dad. I wish my dad didn't hate my mom so much."

Another young woman remembered her sister's trauma and shared it with us:

"It was tough when my sister got married. My family went into great turmoil about who would walk her down the aisle, our dad or our stepdad. See, our dad had never really been her dad, as in father-figure, so she wanted my stepdad to walk her down the aisle. So she told our dad her decision, and it really hurt him and it hurt our grandma, my dad's mom. And they both threatened not to come to the wedding."

One of the topics not uncommon to the "Dear Abby" column is the issue of who, in remarried families, walks the bride down the aisle. Stepfathers, fathers, grandfathers, uncles, and even mothers and stepmothers were all mentioned as loved and appreciated candidates or indignant "rejects" in one series of letters. The agony of the decision was apparent in every letter, as was the deep wish that those considered, those chosen, and those rejected would all lovingly accept and support the decision of the bride. But instead, all too often, from weddings to T-ball games, children report confusion, pain, guilt, and anger because of their parents' inability to be civil, supportive coparents who put the needs and desires of the children first.

It does not have to be this way. It is not necessarily human nature to carry a grudge, seek revenge, and refuse to forgive and move on.

Jungian couples counselor and author, Polly Young-Eisendrath, has written about a yearly event in her family—a nontraditional family reunion. It involves all the ex-spouses, all the "steps," and all the biological relatives who can make it. It is a declaration of extended family and forgiveness. It is an acknowledgment that life goes on, and no matter what, children are wonderful gifts, to be cherished and supported by all who had a hand in their upbringing.

Frankie, a 19-year-old young woman, told us,

"One of the coolest gifts my parents gave me was the times we were all together. I mean, my mom, my dad, both stepparents, four or five grandparents and stepgrandparents, my little sisters, and even one great-grandmother would be together for something of mine—like prom and graduation."

Chloe, a 37-year-old professional woman, related,

"When we held the memorial service for my grandparents, my mother and my ex-stepfather and my stepbrother and my dad and his wife and some cousins by marriages that were no longer marriages and my uncle-in-law all came. And we all honored those wonderful old folks, and all they had done and all they had meant to us. I looked around the room, and for a moment, I felt like my sister and I were being honored, too. All these parent-figures were there, acting concerned about us and even about each other. Too bad it takes such loss to bring people together."

Children realize that after a divorce, everyone isn't one big, happy family. Therefore, those occasions when divorced members of the family get together and treat each other with civility and respect become very precious memories for the children.

THE EVERYDAY STUFF

Possessions

Another common struggle has to do with the material possessions of the children. Clothing, favorite toys or games, bikes, books, even stereos and televisions might be things kids want at each house. Karmen, a 14-year-old, offered this advice:

"Don't be stingy about the kids, and if you want to be stingy, talk on the phone where the kids can't hear it."

Troy, age 15, stated,

"My dad gets mad about me bringing stuff to my mom's; he will ask where the shirt he got for me is and stuff like that. He got me a CD case for Christmas and he said, 'Now I don't want this to disappear to your mom's house,' and I just wanted to scream! He doesn't understand that it is not my fault if something ends up at the black hole of the other house. I wish he would lay off, because he doesn't know what it is like and he is not in a good place to judge and it is my *stuff and they are both* my *houses."*

Material possessions are yet another area that require open co-parenting communication, effective planning, and goodwill. Helping children become responsible for their "things" is fine. However, joint-custody kids firmly believe that their parents have *no idea* what it is like to maintain two residences and shift back and forth frequently. They consistently ask for maturity, assistance, and leniency in the process. They also look to their parents for mature, patient guidance in managing this area. This is the kind of agreement that can be written into parenting plans: "I pledge to treat the gifts and personal items provided by the other parent with care and respect." One person shared with us the following story:

"My parents have let me leave my stuff wherever I want. They buy me stuff and it gets put here and there, but they don't hassle me. We know these people who got a bad divorce when their boy was about a year old. They won't even share the car seat or anything. One time, the mother took his outfit off because it was really cute and expensive and she didn't want him to wear it while his dad had him. And they were screaming at each other in the yard while she took the clothes off of the baby. I'd tell parents who are divorcing to not worry about stuff like that. Who cares? I mean it seems like to the kid that the parents care more about the stuff than the kid."

Parent Meetings

As we mentioned in chapter 2, parent meetings are a very wise way to work on mutual concerns in raising children. All parents face quandaries about how best to help their children develop intellectually, socially, morally, sexually, and so on. Differing styles and values can make some transitions quite difficult, even in intact families. In co-parenting situations, great dedication and tact is called for—always. As Zeke, age 16, shared,

> *"I can't imagine my two parents actually married. They are so different. We all went on a trip to look at colleges, and they drove me nuts. For Christmas this year, my dad bought me a really good book about sex, and when my mom found out about it, she wouldn't talk to him for like 3 months or something, but other than that, they get along pretty well."*

From bedtime to birth control, from savings accounts to sex, it is not terribly likely that divorced parents will entirely agree on how to raise the children. Sometimes, consulting a good family counselor, mediator, parenting coordinator, or other mutually agreed-upon neutral party will be helpful in finding some kind of middle ground and creative compromises. Still, do not put the children in the middle of it all. They hate it. They don't want to referee your battles. More importantly, they don't want to be put in the position of choosing how to raise themselves. A sense of reasonable limits, consistent consequences, a predictable set of expectations, and finally, the feeling that there are adults who love and look out for them—these are all central factors in raising healthy children. Parent meetings and co-parent communication can help immensely toward those goals—if you can manage to keep the goals in mind and the other issues at bay.

DON'T WORK IT OUT THROUGH THE KIDS

Just as meeting, dating, falling in love and marrying have many stages, so does coming apart. At the emotional level, divorcing is a long-term process rather than a single event. Sometimes the divorce literature uses the terms *legal divorce* and *emotional divorce*. Legal divorces may drag on, depending upon settlement issues, but in the end, they have an actual final date, a discernable end. Emotional divorcing is generally a slow process. It takes a long time for people to get over each other. The emotional bonds (both positive and negative) do not simply dissolve when the ink is dry on the court documents. Even in the most amicable divorce, the huge personal, financial, and emotional changes require adjustment time. Often one, or even both, of the partners are still emotionally very connected to the other. Candy, 17, reported of her father,

"He went through weird phases of trying to get my mom back. He joined her church once, and became a leader or something, but it was all a facade. I always have known that my dad still loves my mom, and I used to like that, but now I wish he would find someone that he totally loves and just move on and be happy. It's been 5 years. You'd think he'd get a clue."

Secret keeping is another problem area that surfaces when one parent or the other is not yet emotionally divorced. A 16-year-old boy told us,

"Sometimes my dad still tells me not to tell my mom certain things that he does. But they are totally divorced, why would she care? They both carry an electric information current through me, and they both effect me, and I want them to know the way the other person effects me. I want to be able to say whatever I want, I mean it is my family."

Like many children, this boy hated being asked to keep secrets or to spy and report on the other parent.

Tony, a 17-year-old boy wrote,

"My dad was cheating on my mom, and she found out and broke it off with him. He got so upset, he would come to the house and do cruel things, like disconnect things in her car, and steal things from the house. It's been 8 years, and he takes Mom to court to this day for anything he can. Usually, it's something about custody. Whenever we go to my dad's, I feel like a stranger. He pays no attention to me or my brother. He goes off and works on cars. If he is fighting so much to take us away from our mother, why doesn't he pay more attention to us?"

Tony provides a clear and sad example of using the children to get at the other parent. He and his brother aren't fooled by the constant battles to have custody. It isn't about them. It's about the fact that his father is still hung up on his mother.

Sometimes, people who still haven't attained an "emotional divorce" will do hurtful, irrational things to avoid being anywhere near the other parent. Bernie, whose mother remarried when he was 7 years old, suffered a great deal because his mom and stepdad would not come to his concerts. It wasn't because they didn't have time. It wasn't because they hated music. It was because Bernie's mom couldn't stand to support her son engaging in an activity that her ex-husband loved. Bernie's father was a professional musician, and he was a fanatic about making sure Bernie had lessons, support, and all the other needs a gifted young musician might have. Bernie performed at many concerts, often having a solo spot. Bernie longed for his mother to come once in a while. She never did. She could not overcome her negative connection to her ex-husband. This strong negative connection is an indication of a hang-up in the emotional divorce process. When you need to hurt or deprive your child just so you can act-out against your ex, you are not emotionally disconnected.

Finally, in the realm of parents who are not yet emotionally divorced, some kids told stories of feeling condemned, judged, or even hated because of their resemblance to the other parent. Nicole shared this:

"The worst thing my dad ever yelled at me was 'You are just like your God-damned mother.' I just stared at him. What a stupid thing to say."

A 15-year-old boy said,

"Sometimes, my dad will say 'we're still living in the remains of your mother's gardening' (and he doesn't mean it in a nice way). Or my mother will say that I sound exactly like my dad, and I'm like 'So that's a big sin or something?'"

Certainly, your kids are going to have or develop traits that remind you of their other parent. They might even have the very traits that, in your ex-spouse, nearly drove you nuts before you got the divorce. But despite being "chips off the old block," your children are unique human beings and need love, approval, guidance, limits, and patience as they grow and develop. Flinging your emotional baggage at them will not help them outgrow or alter a few troubling behaviors. Do your children a giant favor and do not compare them to their father or mother.

THE WIDER CIRCLE OF OTHERS

When a divorce occurs, it effects relationships far beyond the two people who are divorcing. As the not-so-funny joke says, divorce turns in-laws into out-laws. It can be quite confusing for children and hard for the grandparents, aunts, uncles, cousins and close family friends, all of whom are affected as well.

In her advice to parents, Leah stressed the importance of staying connected to the extended family members of both parents:

"If you are friends with your ex-husband's extended family, then stay friends with them. At first my mom wouldn't talk to my aunt, my dad's sister, and they used to be really good friends. I really like my aunt and that was really weird."

As Leah's story illustrates, it isn't easy to find a new way to relate to the larger extended family. Divided loyalties take a toll on everyone. In Leah's case, after things settled down, her mother and her father's sister were able to begin rebuilding their relationship. This was a great relief to her.

Ten-year-old Paige reported that her mother was so angry at her father that she tried to turn his whole family against him:

"My mom called my grandma, my dad's mom, and told her that my dad had treated her very bad. I don't think this is a good idea. It made my granny very upset at my mom. I still love going to my granny's house, but now my mom doesn't like it. She says it has to count on my dad's time."

Our society is fragmented enough without divorce denying children the opportunity to develop relationships with their grandparents and other significant elders. Of course, those significant others are well advised to stay neutral about the divorce issues and just enjoy relating to and loving the children.

We received this great story in a letter from a woman in her 20s:

"As I think about good advice to give parents—besides the obvious of getting along and not bad-mouthing each other—I thought of something that has helped me growing up. My father maintained a good relationship with my mother's parents. I realize that his connection to Mom's relatives wasn't broken by the divorce. It reinforced the idea that he wasn't bad, that they

still felt close to him, even though his relationship with my
mother didn't work out. It helped to maintain a sense of family,
rather than splitting apart the extended family."

Having good boundaries is important in surviving many of life's
twists and turns. Extended family members need to remember that
taking sides in a divorce isn't really productive or helpful. In the
strictest sense, a divorce is between two people who made a promise to live faithfully and lovingly together the rest of their lives and
then found they needed to break the promise. This does not auto-
matically dictate any particular course of action for any of the other
adults—whether friends or family.

Another encouraging account was given to us by a woman in her
50s:

"Both my parents made sure that my brother and I spent time
with relatives and family friends. This had the effect of us being
surrounded by many caring people, being made to feel part of
several larger families. By being allowed and encouraged to in-
teract with our extended family, I became particularly close to
my father's sister. She was an unmarried professional woman
who provided a wonderful model of courage and independence
for me."

It may seem trite to repeat this much-touted saying, but it still carries
an important truth. It *does* take a village to raise a child. Divorcing
parents are wise to keep healthy connections going with the wider
circle of relatives and friends, no matter which "side" they originally
came from.

SUMMARY

In this chapter, children of divorce spoke with vigor and emotion.
They want their divorced parents to get along and behave respectfully to each other. From their perspective, it seems so little to ask.
They don't want to be treated like possessions, spies, messengers, or
a means by which one parent can get even with the other parent.

The hardest part to understand is that children want to be allowed
to make up their own minds about their parents. Even if one parent
is far less involved, far less mature or caring, they still don't want the

"better" parent judging or speaking poorly of the other. They report feeling much happier if parents are neutral, or mildly supportive of even less-than-ideal parents.

Furthermore, the children want and need permission to love and be involved with the extended family members of each side of their families. This longing even extends to ex-stepparents and their families. Children come into the world fully equipped and biologically driven to establish long-term loving relationships with their caregivers. It hurts them when they are not allowed or not encouraged to do so.

CHAPTER 4

The New and Improved Parent

No matter who initiates a divorce, most parents feel quite concerned about the effect it will have on the children. If you are the parent who is being divorced, that is, if you didn't want the divorce, you might find yourself condemning the other parent both for rejecting you and for hurting the children. You might fall prey to the temptation to voice your disappointment, hatred, and condemnation of the other parent to the children. You may also feel so devastated and emotionally raw that you begin to feel you have nothing to offer the children. Their demands and needs may seem overwhelming. You may feel your self-esteem slipping and your bitterness overcoming your better parental judgments.

On the other hand, if you are the one who decided to pursue a divorce, choosing to divorce the mother or father of your children can feel like a cruel thing to do to your children. It can shake your parental self-image. Society tends to agree with your self-condemnation, which only makes things worse. You might believe you need to justify your choice by stating terrible things about the children's other parent. You might feel you need to prove your love for the children by fighting to have them live with you, or you might feel like such a jerk that you quietly bow out of their lives. You may, in other words, overcompensate or undercompensate for your perceived failings.

We have some important, good news for parents struggling with guilt and resentment. It comes in three parts. First, recent solid social science research reveals that most children—about 75%—are essentially unharmed by their parents' divorce. This doesn't mean it's easy or painless, but most children are not permanently damaged. Second, children from high-conflict families often show improvements in their behavior following their parents' divorce. Actually having the courage to divorce and get it over with when the situation is destructive can be a good thing for children. Third, the single most important factor for children's positive adjustment is having at least one adult (whether it be a mother, father, member of the extended family, or family friend) with whom children have a stable emotional connection and predictable, caring relationship.

The bottom line here is that, even after divorce, the possibility exists of new, improved relationships with your children. A stable, emotionally healthy relationship is worth working and fighting for, and this fact was echoed in the comments from children we surveyed.

One young respondent told us,

"When I was five my dad was always at work and never home with me and my mom, I guess because they were going to get a divorce and he didn't like being with my mom a lot. I never, ever saw him. Now I get to go visit him at his apartment and he plans fun trips and we play games and he takes me to dinner, and when I see him he is happier and we have fun."

Children recognize when their parents are unhappy or estranged from each other. Often after a divorce, parents are happier and more centered on their children, and the children like the individual attention they get. Some of our respondents reported this to be an enriching experience.

This chapter, despite it coverage of several grim topics, can be a hopeful chapter for divorced or divorcing parents. As one 21-year-old respondent aptly stated,

"You can be a good parent or a bad parent whether you are divorced or not."

Divorce might be one of the most challenging times in the life of a parent, but it can be a time of opportunity rather than simply a time of loss. There are ways that divorced parents can actually capitalize on being divorced and make it part of becoming a better parent than they ever were before. But first, here are some basic warnings.

Don't take it out on the dog
or the kids!

NO DISPLACEMENT

*"Parents, don't take your anger out on the kids. And after you
are separated, spend time with your kids and go kind of easy on
them. Don't get depressed all the time, and get out and explore
things,"*
said one 13-year-old boy. You probably don't need to be told this, but
children, like the family dog, do not want to have your anger or bad
mood taken out on them. In "psychobabble," this is called displace-
ment. It happens when we do not express our emotional reactions to
the person or people who caused the emotional reaction and instead, we stuff it until we express it, at the slightest provocation, to
someone smaller or less powerful than we are.

A very mature thing parents must do is almost the opposite of dis-
placement. They must behave themselves even when they don't feel
like it. They must delay the gratification of their needs in the service
of offering a wise, loving, mature role model to their children. As this
11-year-old girl said,

*"Parents should behave around their kids or at least try because
it will be a lot easier for the kids."*

NO USE OF CHILDREN AS BUDDIES OR COUNSELORS

"I think it is important after a divorce for parents to be independent to a certain extent. Kids go through enough without having to make sure their parents are doing okay, or feeling guilty about doing stuff on their own,"

a 14-year-old girl told us. Emotional support is sometimes lacking for divorcing parents, and they may turn to their children for it. Bad move. Over and over again, children and adult children of divorce told us that they did *not* want to be their parents' best friends. They did *not* want to know their parents' fears or secrets. They did *not* want to stay home to keep a newly single parent company. They did *not* want to be the emotional representative for their other parent or for all men or women in the world. You might want to review a few of the quotes in chapter 1. A number of respondents remembered being burdened and traumatized by carrying their parents' emotional burdens. Children of divorce can adjust to divorce and to all that comes with it much more easily if they are assured of their ongoing role in the family—that of being dependent, growing, developing children.

NO USE OF CHILDREN AS SUBSTITUTE PARENTS

Similar to the error of using children for friends is the error of expecting them to step in and fill the shoes of the missing parent. Josh noticed a change in his work around the house as he adjusted to life with only one parent at a time:

"It seems like after the divorce my mom máde me do a lot more stuff because my dad was gone. I had a lot of chores around the house, but not as many as my brother, maybe because he was older."

The parentified child is a well-known problem in family counseling circles. It doesn't just happen in divorced families. It happens in addicted families and families in which one parent is weak or emotionally absent. It happens in big families in which there isn't enough time or money to go around. And when it happens to the extreme, it is damaging.

A parentified child is a different thing than children who assume certain age-appropriate responsibilities within the family structure. Children can be asked to help out a great deal without doing them any harm. However, they should not be asked to assume the worries, concerns, and final authority that should rest with parents. They should not be left to feel that the health and well-being of family members is entirely up to them. And they should, as children, never be asked to serve as the parent, advisor, or soulmate to their own parent.

Children can understand and accept the need to take on a few extra responsibilities if that is necessary for family well-being. The assignments should be carefully thought out, and the parent should take time to explain that there are now fewer people in the house but the same amount of work needing to be done. Be careful. The choice to use the children to do more of the homemaking, vehicle maintenance, yard work, and babysitting can easily go too far. Parentified or adultified children feel resentful and overburdened as children and ripped off as adults.

PROTECT THAT OLDEST CHILD

Birth order is a much-debated aspect of family identity. Do oldest children end up as leaders more often? Are middle children likely to be peacemakers? Will the youngest grow up to demand special attention? We leave the answers to the social scientists. Quite a number of our children of divorce told us clearly that they believed the oldest child took the divorce the hardest. Obviously, this won't be the case every time, but since it was mentioned quite frequently, it seems worth noting.

Parents should perhaps pay careful attention that they do not shrug off responsibility onto the oldest child simply because he or she is available. Moms and dads also should take extra time to talk to the oldest child, because he or she is often the child that understands and grieves the most throughout the divorce. Jenny, a 13-year-old girl who was 3 at the time of her parents' divorce, told us,

"You really should talk to my older brother. He had to do more chores, really hates my stepmom and took everything way harder than I did."

It was a very common observation, both by children who were the oldest and by their younger siblings.

IT'S OKAY TO HAVE RULES AND VALUES

In times of transition or crisis, our normal routines sort of implode on themselves. It is hard to reorient and get new routines stabilized. Children have the reputation of taking advantage of disrupted times and guilt-ridden parents, and certainly some do. But many other don't. They just quietly go about rebuilding their worlds the best they can. At any rate, it is important to realize that all social groups need rules and rituals, and families are no exception. Bedtime observed, teeth brushed, dished cleared, curfew obeyed, car used responsibly, allowance earned, TV limits observed, and other rules all need to be as routine and steady as possible. Consequences need to stay consistent as well.

Sometimes parents' feelings of guilt or dismay over the divorce can cause them to lighten up on the usual guidance and family rules. They assume by "going easy" on the kids, they are helping them heal or are making up for the fact that they are a divorced family. A 16-year-old girl whose parents divorced when she was 4 told us,

> *"I stayed with my dad mostly. Looking back, I can't believe what he let me do. I was out of control and wild by the time I was in middle school. Then we moved, and he got involved with this woman, Jeanne, and she was really into limits. She told my dad that she thought I needed limits, and my dad agreed, I guess. And it helped me. I kind of wanted to change anyway, but I went from being a party freak to getting good grades and playing sports and even cheerleading. I feel like I made the decisions to change myself, to some extent, but it helped that Dad was trying to know what I was up to and stuff."*

This girl's father "woke up" before it was too late, and he was there to help her reign things in a little.

Some parents feel threatened because the other parent chooses to be more lenient, either naturally or as a result of the divorce, and is therefore considered to be "a whole lot more fun." The other parent throws out the rules, buys pizzas and R-rated videos, makes extravagant promises, and takes the easy road at every turn. This is difficult and painful for the more responsible parent. Adult support, parenting classes, and sometimes, mediation or some other kind of third-party assistance is needed.

Sometimes, because one parent seems to be lenient, the other parent becomes reactively more strict. Kurt, a 12-year-old boy, told us,

"When we were at my mom's we could stay up as late as we wanted, and my dad hated that. He would hear about it and get mad and make us go to bed earlier than ever at his house. He is a pretty controlling guy. If he wasn't so controlling, I would like to do more things with him. We hunt and fish together and that's fun, but my dad has a temper, and that is no fun."

You can't "parent away" the other parent's deficits by overcompensating. If all they get at the other parent's house are hamburgers, soda pop, and chocolate, don't make the mistake of serving all vegetables. Sure, serve some veggies and some tuna casserole, but it's okay to have treats. Don't let the other parent's failings tighten you up and make you lose your own natural fun, spontaneity, joy, and generosity.

Most children can sense when they are being treated ingenuously. One 16-year-old girl told us,

"My parents are a lot nicer than they ever were when they were married, but I don't think it will last. They are doing the competition thing for being the nicer parent. They weren't bad before, anyway."

Although our respondents were not too keen on "fake-nice" parenting, many noted the pleasure involved in watching their parents find new lives and happier times, as illustrated in the following quote:

"The only reason I'm glad my parents got together is that they had me. But they were a bad match. My mom was really shy and my dad pushed her and made her feel insecure instead of helping. And my dad was lonely all the time because my mom didn't like outdoor things or sports. Now he has a girlfriend who is totally outgoing and loves to hike and stuff, and Mom is going back to school and meeting people on her own. She's going to be a teacher and I think she'll be excellent."

A SCORNED OR FAVORED PARENT

It is true, as we stated in chapter 2, that children generally want to know and be loved by both of their parents. Nonetheless, many go through times of wanting distance from a given parent. This can be a trying situation for the preferred parent as well as the resisted parent. The age of the child and the reasons given for the resistance need to be carefully considered.

> *"My mom loves my retarded brother more than me. I can't stand to be at her house. All I do is work. I have to rake the yard, do the dishes, even brush my brother's dog. She barely notices if I'm there except for the list of things she has for me to do. I don't even want to be there on weekends. And she can't make me."*

This 13-year-old boy's parents were just recently divorced when we spoke with him. He had made his wishes known to counselors, lawyers, and anyone who would listen. He wanted to live with his dad, and he did not want to be around his mother or his developmentally disabled younger brother. Clearly, there is a lot of emotional work to do in this family, but forcing the boy to live half the time with his mother only makes things worse. This boy's mom *and* dad need to find a way to help him reconnect with and appreciate his mother and come to terms with the needs his brother places on the family system, but it will be a gradual process. In the meantime, it will likely be painful and frustrating for his mother.

Sometimes, the child can be gently encouraged to at least spend a little time and work things through with the resisted parent. A counselor or mutual friend can be asked to help, too. Forcing the issue if the child is adamant can be quite damaging. Parents who patiently weather a situation in which a child expresses a desire for distance are very wise. It is better to let a child have some space than to force him or her to spend time with the parent in question. Kayla, age 18, told us,

> *"My parents were pretty laid back about where my brother and I were staying, except for one thing. We were not allowed to go stay with the one parent if we were mad at the other, or if we were grounded or in trouble or something. We could switch, but we couldn't switch until we got over being grounded or worked*

*out our feelings. Mostly, I think this is a good plan, but some-
times I used to hate it."*

Children in fully functional, intact families often go through natural times of feeling closer to one parent than the other. It isn't easy
for the less preferred parent, but it is certainly less threatening than
when the same natural preference occurs in a divorced family. One
respondent shared,

*"When I was little, my dad was about the neatest thing in the
world to me. I cried to be with him on Mom's weeks and I can
remember trying to tell her I liked her too, but I wanted my
daddy. I don't remember Mom getting mad at me, but I know
now that it hurt her. When I was with my dad, we'd go on neat
trips and he'd try to find ways to have me stay longer. I loved it.
But then, in high school, I was closer to my mom for some reason. My dad had a hard time with the switch."*

Parenting is a complex task, to say the least. We can derive great
satisfaction from being close and connected to our children. It can
feel wonderful to be preferred, and devastating to be less preferred
or even scorned or ignored. Letting children prefer their other parent, or even a stepparent, over us without acting out our hurt or becoming defensive, takes a lot of support and maturity, and a great
deal of courage. Certainly, you can impose consequences for acting
disrespectfully, but demanding that your children love you, or con-
triving ways to control them or get even, will only make matters
worse. Patient, steady, unconditional love is a large part of the answer. Also, seeking other sources of fulfillment, and thus creating a
little healthy detachment can also help.

It is also quite taxing to do the right thing when you are the preferred parent. Encouraging a child to forgive someone you don't
even like is hard to do. Trying to help a child be tolerant or understanding of the other parent's failings, when inside you feel anything
but tolerant or understanding, is a monumental task. And of course,
in some situations, you should not work to have the children con-
nect to the other parent (we discuss this further in chapter 7). But
most of the time, learning to keep loving both parents, shortcomings,
disappointments and all, is an important part of growing up.

A very angry 17-year-old boy told us,

"Yeah, I used to be at my dad's about 50% of the time, but that f— — S.O.B. let his girlfriend start acting like she was some kind of parent to me, and she made up a bunch of stupid rules and he stuck by her. We had a fight that was so bad I just ran away for 3 days and no one knew where I was. He changed the locks on his house. I won't ever stay there again, and I don't care if I ever see him again either."

This boy's parents both have their work cut out for them. They'll need time, patience, tolerance, limits, and forgiveness, but the direction needs to be toward gradually working it out so the relationships are rebuilt.

Another reason children may begin to resist spending time with parents is that they need and want more social time with their peers. The lives of many American teens are full to the bursting point with homework, sports, music, and social activities. Squeezing time in for two separate parent relationships can feel like too much. This can be especially challenging if one parent lives at a distance.

Sixteen-year-old Mandy said,

"My dad refused to listen to me. I wanted to see him, but not so often. And I didn't mind traveling to see his parents, my grandparents, either. But he wouldn't pay for a plane ticket and so it was going to take a week of driving, just with him. I have a job, friends, homework, and piano. I got so sick of his demands, I just told him I didn't want to see him at all. Not even at my recitals. But he came anyway. I was furious. What an ass. He thinks he has a right to intrude in my life whatever way he wants. He just keeps insisting I spend all 'his' time with him. It's my time and my life. I want nothing to do with him, and if he tries to push it, I will tell the court that too."

Mandy's situation calls for a kind of creative maturity that apparently her father has not yet developed. Relationships can be deep and meaningful and still not take incredible amounts of time, but that requires a lot of effort on the parent's part. After early adolescence, negotiating directly with the children about how to spend time together and how to enhance the relationship is a real possibility. The parental perspective should include a recognition of the needs and social demands in the teenager's life. If the relationship is already shaky, using a family counselor as a mediator might be helpful.

SPECIAL ISSUES OF GAY AND LESBIAN PARENTS

Being a homosexual parent offers challenges beyond those already covered in this book. Bobby, a man in his 20s, said,

"My real mom was an abusive batterer. Thank God my dad got me away from her. He married Lucy, the woman I consider to be my mom, and we had a decent life for quite a few years. Then Lucy admitted she was gay. She and Dad got a divorce, but I lived with her a lot of the time and I still stay there quite a bit. She has a partner, but they don't live together. Since my dad died, I consider Lucy my closest family. It doesn't bother me that she's gay because she loves me, and that's what has always mattered."

The challenges and developmental issues faced by gay or lesbian parents are beyond the scope of this book, but one thing is clear. Both homosexual and heterosexual people can make great, stable, loving homes for their children and both can fail to do so. Being gay doesn't seem to be the issue. Being a good parent does. We list a couple of resources that can be helpful for gay or lesbian parents in the last chapter.

FORGIVE YOURSELF (AND THE OTHER) AND MOVE ON

A 63-year-old woman told us about her parents' divorce:

"Back then, divorce was just unheard of. My father was the one who left. He didn't stay in touch. My mother was quite ashamed, and so was I. It's better nowadays, I think. Less stigma. But there's still some there. It's still a failure, I think. But it's better to pick up and go on with life. We all make mistakes, and no one really has the right to judge us. Back then, we were pretty harshly judged."

Divorcing parents can't do much about the judgments others will level at them, but they can choose to forgive themselves and go on with their lives.

No one wants the defining feature of their household to be that of divorce. One child told us,

"The way my dad likes to get us feeling guilty is to tell us how lonely he is when we are at Mom's. He hates the house he's in and how broke he feels and it's about all he can talk about. When we bring friends over, my dad likes to explain our whole family history. It's been over a year now and I wish we could get on with it."

This child's father is having trouble moving on. He's spending time with his children, but it sounds like he's a one-trick pony right now—relating most of his current life back to the divorce.

As our elders will tell us, the years go by with amazing speed. Our children are only children for such a short, precious time. It is tragic to waste part of that wonderful, formative time pouting and revisiting adult disappointments and resentments on the heads of our children. Children can use all sorts of attention. There are silly, intriguing, or educational games to play. There are long walks to take. There are school projects. There are child-based important things to talk over—like the relative merits of mountain bikes, baggy pants, tattoos, and pierced tongues. There are pets to care for. There are things to grow in the garden. There is music to listen to. There are things to learn together. There are short and long excursions to plan. There are meals to cook. There are languages to learn. There are neighborhood projects to help with. There are plays to act in. Okay, you get the idea.

As 14-year-old Jamal said,

"If you're gonna get a divorce, remember that the children are the most important thing. Think of them first, not your own anger, or your own hurt, but them. It is really hard, but that is the key to a successful divorce, if there is such a thing."

HELP THE CHILDREN LEARN

Sometimes, parents can give their children a very great gift by sharing the story of their own struggles and failures. Naturally, children learn by example, but they also learn by the honest assessment their parents make of themselves. Juanita, a young woman, told us,

"It's interesting to note how I am not repeating some of my parents' mistakes, because they were so open about them. I guess if you are open, you can help your kids avoid the mistakes you made. You can bet I'm going to try."

The children we interviewed were open and ready to talk. Having been through hard times gave them insight into their own hurts, fears, and strengths. Divorced parents have the obligation and the opportunity to help their children heal in a way that, in the end, might make them stronger. As this young woman, about to finish high school, shared,

"I know my relationships with guys are always fleeting because I'm scared of abandonment or betrayal. I also have a fuzzy view of what a healthy marriage should be. I'm afraid of commitment and concrete decisions. These are all things that have subconsciously been instilled in me because of divorce."

Even now, years after the divorce, it is clear that she is still sorting things out. Honest, caring discussion with both parents would be the best possible prescription for her.

THE BEST THAT YOU CAN BE

As a divorced parent, you are on your own to establish or reestablish ways of relating to each of your children.

"My dad is not even the same person he was before the divorce. He listens to me. We got a dog. I'd say to parents, well, this is your chance to change. Maybe you weren't so good as a parent because you weren't so happy while you were married. But now, like my dad, you can be with your kids more."

This 12-year-old boy went on to explain that his dad was even making rules, and helping with homework, and doing all sorts of things that only his mother had done before. The child was clearly enjoying this new relationship with his father.

A young woman in her 20s told us,

"My parents divorced when I was a toddler. It was my mom's second divorce. My dad wasn't in the picture much at all as I

I think kids really want a family whith two parents. My Mom lives in another town She goes to school, and Some times people tease me about that. I'm kind of mad at my mom for not talking to me and my little brother and my big brother (I sugest that moms or dads talk to thar kids)

grew up. He remarried, but he didn't have kids, so basically, he never raised any kids. I would like for him to know my girls now, and be a grandfather to them, and I think he would like that, too. But he doesn't know how to relate. I wish he'd stayed involved in my growing up years."

This father's choice will reverberate for at least another generation. For whatever reasons, he didn't find a way to stay in a relationship with his daughter and actively parent her as she grew. She missed out, he missed out, and now another generation is in danger of missing out. The basic message is, "Hang in there." Do what is humanly possible to stay involved in parenting your children.

One girl, in her late teens, told us about watching the changes in her mother after the divorce:

"My mom positively blossomed. She started taking classes and talking to me about things I was learning in school and stuff. It was amazing. I don't think I would feel the same way about her if they hadn't divorced. I didn't know her, or maybe she actually changed."

Children benefit from having happy, active, well-adjusted parents who pay attention to their children and share significant portions of life with them.

One understanding but disappointed child of divorce shared,

"When parents first start realizing there's going to be a divorce, I think they have good intentions of being good parents, of keeping in touch, and stuff. But then time goes by, and good intentions get discarded—time, money, issues like that. It isn't easy to keep the good intentions going."

Other adult occupations have tried to lay claim to being the world's oldest profession, but we believe parenting actually gets the award. Humans have needed attentive, loving parents for a long, long time. Unfortunately, this does not mean that parenting is necessarily a natural, inborn skill. Studies have shown that primates separated from their parents and raised in peer groups don't seem to know how to parent their offspring. Studies have also shown that we tend to parent our children the way our parents did us, but that we can *choose* to parent differently. All of these findings suggest that a large component of parenting is learned. This is good news. It means that parenting, as a learned skill, can always be improved. The choice is always available to learn more and get even better at it. Divorce can provide the stimulus for you to seek more parenting skills—through groups, classes, counseling, or good readings. As the overused but challenging saying goes, when life hands you lemons, make lemonade. Divorce, for most people, qualifies as lemons. Becoming a better parent than you ever were before could, well. . . dare we say it? You decide. It's up to you, but there's nothing quite as tasty as good lemonade.

One of our respondents put it this way:

"What I think parents should do when they get divorced is just keep on loving their kids. Try as hard as a mother or father can

to help their kids along with the divorce because they are the ones getting hurt the most. Never make a child feel guilty for a choice they made. Love them either way. Even if they choose to live with the other parent. Do things like call all the time and keep communicating. That is the best thing to do when you are in this situation. Let the child always know you are just a phone call away and let them know you love them."

SUMMARY

Sometimes, divorced parents need to recreate a relationship with their children, and generally, children welcome this process. They want healthy, happy parents who take an interest in their lives. Children don't want to be their parents' buddies or counselors. They don't want to be a substitute for the other parent. They need structure, predictability, flexibility, and downtime.

As children develop and mature, their needs within the child-to-adult relationship change. They may need or want less time, or they may want to do different activities. Wise parents do not demand relationships on their own adult terms with their children. They listen and calibrate the amount of time spent, and the types of activities, so that they aren't burdening the children with parental needs. Parenting as a divorced person has challenges and difficulties, but there are also opportunities for exciting new improvements as well.

CHAPTER 5

Dating, Romance, and Recommitment

For many of the children we spoke with, the idea of one of their parents dating someone new was startling at first. The whole notion took some getting used to for them. Shannon, whose parents divorced when she was 5 years old, can still remember how strange it felt when her mom's date bought her an ice cream cone a few months after the divorce was final:

> *"He rubbed my head and told me I was a cute kid and gave me a bubble gum ice cream cone—my favorite flavor. But I remember thinking 'You're not my dad. Don't rub my head,' and I started crying. Mom was really embarrassed."*

To overcome the startled feelings and the embarrassment, the best advice kids have to offer parents is to *communicate clearly and proceed slowly*. Even small children can understand if mommy or daddy is going to spend time with someone special, but they need time to think it through and talk about it. They need to understand that their parents are no longer going to be with each other romantically. They need to understand that the commitment to fidelity is over. It is hard to find words to explain this to young children, but it is important to try. You can say something like, "Honey, Mommy and Daddy aren't married anymore. When people are married, they love each other and they spend special time together. Your Mommy and I aren't going to do that any more. Each of us might find some other grown-ups to do things with and to be our special friends. Your Mommy knows that I might go out and do things with some other women, and I know that she might go out with some other men. We both understand that because that is part of what it means to get a divorce."

Older children can be told more directly. One child reported the following story:

"My mom has always been open and honest with me about sex. After Dad moved out, Mom asked me how I would feel if she brought a date home. I said I wasn't quite ready and she said, 'That's cool,' and she didn't force me to be accepting of it. I knew she was interested in this one guy, and he was a nice guy too, but I was so glad she didn't make me be around or act like it was normal to have dinner with them or something."

Besides the obvious adjustments and discomforts associated with parents dating, it is quite common for children to harbor the fantasy that their parents will get back together. Their objection to parental dating may be in part due to the hope that the parents will soon want to begin dating each other. It helps everyone move along and adjust if parents are gently honest about this aspect of divorce. Certainly, some people choose not to date anyone after a divorce, but for those who are going to date, a chat with the children is in order.

Introducing dating and the actual people you date into the lives of children should be done slowly, respectfully, and with caution. From the stories and feelings our interview participants shared with us, it seems best to keep the social life separate when it is at the casual date level. Children certainly don't have to meet everyone with whom their parents go out for coffee. Later, of course, if things are getting serious, the kids need to be welcomed into the growing relationship, but this should not be done too soon, and the children should not be too involved. And as always, communication is key to making things easier, as this quote illustrates:

"The hardest thing was when my parents got new people. All of a sudden, my mom's boyfriend moved in with us. I couldn't adjust to that. It would have been better if my mom talked to me about it, and it gradually happened."

Children and adult children of divorce expressed a preference for parents with modesty and discretion in their dating lives, but not to the point of secrecy. If your boyfriend or girlfriend is going to sleep over, children would prefer to know what is expected of them. A frank discussion would be welcome—in contrast to hiding or pretending. One boy told us,

"My dad has had like five girlfriends, but only the first one ever stayed over when we were around. My dad sleeps on a futon, and one night, after we were in bed, we could hear the wood creaking and stuff. My sister told my mom about it, and I guess she called my dad, and since then, he hasn't had anyone stay the night while we were there."

Marcy, a 13-year-old girl, shared this story:

"At first, it was weird with Roger, because we were really good friends with his family, and with their kids who are our age, and with their whole family. And then, it kind of drifted, and then all of a sudden my mom was hanging out with Roger a lot, and I didn't know that Roger and his wife were divorced until my mom told me. It was hard at first, but now I just call him my stepdad, because I doubt they will marry since my mom has been through two marriages and is not too keen on the idea. I think she did a good job of handling it, though. She told me that they were going to see each other. She just asked if I was okay with it. I thought it was bound to happen, and they are perfect together. I dealt with it knowing that if she was happy with him, then I would rather have her happy and me deal with it than have her restrict her life to what makes the kids happy."

KIDS AS BAIT

Another point made many times in the interviews and in essays provides the title for this section: Don't use the children as bait!

"When my stepdad and mom started dating, my mom would make me try to act like the perfect kid. She wanted me to impress him, but I didn't care about him and I didn't even want to try. It was like I had to be someone different to help her catch this guy."

An episode of a top-rated TV show featured two of the male characters borrowing their friend's child to attract "chicks." The notion of pretending to have cute, bright children as a come-on is a bit novel, but wanting children you *aren't* borrowing to be charming, unusually well-groomed, and on their best behavior isn't probably all that uncommon. And children don't especially like it.

Tammy, a precocious 14-year-old, told us,

"Advise all parents to leave you out of their love lives. My dad asked me to babysit this woman's bratty little kid so he could go out with her. And I was supposed to buy him treats and act all cool and impress him. He was a hyperactive snotty-nosed demon. I finally shut him in his room. No kidding. And did I ever catch hell. He never dated that woman again though."

KIDS AS TURN-OFFS

A common stereotype is that being a parent makes you less attractive to eligible romantic partners. Children have radar that lets them know instantly if you are ashamed of them or perceive them as a burden. Colleen, now 27 years old, got the distinct impression that her father would rather he didn't have children and could just start over. She told us,

"He'd ship us off to his mother's house whenever he had a date. Sometimes, he'd go out with a woman for months and I bet he never mentioned us."

KIDS AS DATE SPIES

As we mentioned in chapter 3, children also reported being "pumped" for information by one parent about the other parent's dating habits. This is a very bad idea. It's inappropriate, embarrassing, and developmentally damaging to children. They mostly hated being caught in the middle, but some admitted feeling kind of cool at the time, spying on Mom and reporting to Dad. Later, though, they felt shame and disgust.

GETTING SERIOUS (OR WHO'S THE BOSS? PART I)

Parental authority over children is assumed to be the natural right of adoptive or biological parents. It is not the right of just any adult, and it is very definitely not a right earned by an adult because he or she happens to date someone's mom or dad. Children expressed clear and justified resentment toward adults who assumed because they'd spent the night with a parent, they could boss the kids around the next day. Even Mom or Dad's steady girl- or boyfriend does not have parental rights and should treat children with respect, deferring to the children's parent if there is a need for discipline.

Jordan was a 7-year-old boy who was very close to his mother. His dad lived most of the year in another country, so Jordan didn't know his father well. His mother dated casually off and on, finally settling into a steady dating relationship with Ted. Jordan shared the following:

"Ted is not the boss of me. He tells me what to do and I tell my mom on him, but sometimes she makes me do what he says."

In chapter 4, we told of one respondent who completely left his father's home because his father's girlfriend started trying to lay down her own version of the law, and the young man felt betrayed and furious when his father stood up for the girlfriend. Generally, it is a serious mistake for even stepparents to assume authoritative roles in children's lives without a lot of careful relationship building and trust. It is even more of a mistake for boyfriends or girlfriends to take on parental authority.

Certainly, children should be expected to treat adults with respect. They should be attentive and kind to aunts, uncles, grandparents, and adult neighbors and friends of the family. Therefore, they can be expected to treat their parent's boyfriend or girlfriend with respect and kindness. They should not be expected, however, to obey parental guidance or commands from even a serious, live-in boyfriend or girlfriend. Parents should not put romantic partners in a position to "parent" the children. From what our respondents shared, it seems a recipe for disaster, and is not worth it.

REMARRIAGE

An 8-year-old girl shared this sage advice, shown in original form on page 92:

"I think you shouldn't marry too soon after the big D. You should wait until you and your child are ready to move on."

I Think that you should'ent meary to soon after the big D. you should wate intel you and your cild is ready to move on

It seems ideal to let things heal and take time getting adjusted to being a divorced family before becoming a remarried family, but of course, that isn't always the way things work. Remarriage of a divorced parent is not easy for most children, but parental choices can make it much better... or much worse.

"My dad made a horrible mistake. He gave us totally no warning. I mean, geez, he'd dated a different woman every month and kept it all his own business. But then, wham, he just decides he's found someone to marry and brought her home and she moved it. Just like that. I mean, tell parents this: 'Give us time.' These people can't just appear in our lives and become our relatives!"

This advice was offered by 13-year-old Courtney, whose father had dated casually for a few years but then suddenly, in the span of less than a month, he announced he was in love and soon to marry. The woman moved into the house. Courtney had only met her twice and neither time did they really have a chance to get acquainted. It was shocking that her father was calling this woman his fiancée. Courtney was indignant and resistant. What could have been a nice addition to her life became a power struggle between her and her father. He didn't do it right, and she was going to let him know—by rejecting this woman, maybe forever.

Tim, whose mother was moving to another town to be with her boyfriend, stated,

> *"I assume they are going to get married because they are moving in together, but I don't know, I guess my mom will just call me and say. Really, parents should let their kids know exactly what is going on."*

Sam, age nine, offered the following wise advice:

> *"Wait a while before you get married so the kids can get to know the new stepmom. I didn't know my dad was getting married until he just did."*

Sometimes, as in Courtney's case, children feel as if their parents have just married a complete stranger. It seems quite understandable that children would want and need time to get acquainted with someone who is going to assume an important role in the rest of their lives. This may be difficult for emotional or logistical reasons, but from what we heard from our respondents, it is well worth the sacrifice.

On the other hand, sometimes, as in Marcy's situation described previously, parents get romantically involved with family friends or someone else the children know. Casey reported every teenager's nightmare:

> *"Mrs. Arnold was one of our teachers and when they started dating, my brother started hating her. When they told us they were going to get married my brother made my dad take him to my mom's. He was so mad. She wasn't a bad person or anything. It was just embarrassing. You don't want your dad going and marrying your teacher."*

Children's reports about their parents' remarriage process tended to go one of two ways. Either they felt included and enthused, enjoying helping with the plans involved in this new arrangement, or they felt resentful, confused, shy, and left out. Obviously, this is a place where parents and their new romantic partners can make important choices. They can work hard to communicate and provide plenty of adjustment time and relationship-building energy, and perhaps sway events toward a very positive direction. Of course, not all children will choose to endorse their parent's remarriage, no matter what is done, but the vast majority want to be respected, informed, and involved.

Kids fear that they will lose the attention or love of their parents when new family members are brought in without explanation or consideration. As Brett pointed out,

"It took me a long time to realize that you can have different kinds of relationships. Let your kids know there are two different kinds of love. And take time out to do stuff with just your kid again, because they are used to doing stuff with just you."

The good news was that some of those who felt shock or resentment told us that later they accepted the situation and were happy to have the new person in their lives, as 14-year-old Jason stated:

"At first it was hard, but then I started thinking about the good things about my mom having a boyfriend. They are so happy and she is happy all the time. She goes camping and hiking and running, and her boyfriend is wonderful."

SUMMARY

In this chapter, we covered the views of our respondents about their parents dating or getting into another romantic relationship. Their advice boils down to three important points:

1. Be respectful of the children. Don't let your date try to boss the kids around, and don't use the kids to get dates.
2. Go slowly and carefully.
3. Be honest and keep everyone informed.

CHAPTER 6

Stepparenting

Tracey was 4 years old when her parents divorced, and 6 when her dad remarried. She told us,

> *"Going through the divorce wasn't the worst part, but when my father remarried to my stepmother it was rough going. So if you could just have a chapter about how to treat stepchildren fairly...."*

Well, Tracey, here it is. We agree with you and a whole lot of other concerned children of divorce. This is an important issue. Being a stepfamily isn't easy. There aren't many fairytales that feature a warm, loving stepparent and grateful, happy, well-adjusted stepchildren. It may be time for some new fairytales.

FORGET THE RESCUE FANTASIES

Sometimes, divorced parents believe that by remarrying, they can make things all better again. Sometimes, stepparents allow themselves to think they can somehow fix things, too. Neither is a good motive for marriage, and neither is likely to be true. Cameron, a 13-year-old girl, stated the following:

> *"It's never the same as your original family. My stepdad came along, but it didn't really make my family feel whole again. My sister and I didn't feel like we were an instant new family, but I guess it was the right direction. It helped a little."*

95

Dan, whose parents divorced when he was 3 years old, said,

"Mom was desperate to find someone to be a father figure to me. I only saw my dad about every 2 years. She dated this awful guy, Bobby. He was determined to make me into a man. I was only about 6. Thank God she didn't stick with him. Later, we moved and she met Max, and Max is cool. I mean, he cares and he has good ideas and he's steady. He's not my dad, but he's an okay guy."

Most of our respondents did not feel happy or excited about the addition of a stepparent into their lives. As this 14-year-old said,

"I feel that having a stepparent is like being in a new and strange world. Your real parent is different that he or she has been, and the stepparent is a manipulator of the new world in which he or she is in control. Being in this position, it is hard to cope, but you must go on."

Mona, a mother in her early 20s, said,

"People who divorce are likely to divorce again, you know. I came from my mom's second marriage. She's on her fourth now. So why would anyone be excited about a stepparent if it might mean going through a divorce again? I won't get a divorce if there's any way at all to avoid it. I don't want my children thinking marriage is easy. It is all about sacrifice. Hopefully, they won't think marriage is a piece of cake, and then end up disillusioned."

WHO'S THE BOSS? PART II

We made a strong claim in chapter 5 about the lines of parental authority. Basically, we said that parental authority is *parental* authority and should remain pretty strictly with the biological or adoptive parents. What about after marriage? What about when you are all living together under the same roof? Shouldn't the stepparent have parental authority then? From what the respondents told us, our answer would be a qualified "no." However, stepparents can slowly earn the right to have what might be called stepparental authority.

RELATIONSHIP—FIRST, LAST, AND ALWAYS

If you choose to marry someone with children, thus becoming a stepparent, you have a very important assignment: Build a good relationship with those children. They may resist your overtures. They may ignore you, infuriate you, or make you very, very sad. They might even frighten you. It is still your job to build a good relationship with those children. Or at least to try with everything you have in you. You may think, "Well, shouldn't they have to meet me half way?" No. They didn't ask to have you in their lives. They have reasons to be cautious. They have reasons to distrust relationships and adults. And they may get all sorts of pressure from within and without to distance themselves from you. As the adult, you are the one who must go many extra miles.

Melissa pointed out the pieces of her relationship with her stepmother, some that were good and some that were hard:

"I get along with her when we are just talking to each other, like when I am just talking to her as Beth, not as my dad's wife, but then when she tries to control me and make parent-like decisions she makes me crazy. My advice to stepparents is build a relationship with the kids, don't use them to get close to the other person. Don't try to have so much parental power right off the bat. Try to be their friend first."

Researchers have shown that healthy, happy human relationships contain many, many more positive, affirmative interactions than confrontations or criticisms between the people in the relationship. They suggest a good rule of thumb for healthy relationships: five to one. *For every single critical or confrontive comment made, there should be at least five positive ones made first.* It isn't a bad idea to try for 10! This is an especially good rule for new stepparents. It may be all too easy to want to take control or to offer critical input. Stay positive. Build the relationship first.

SLOW, STEADY, GRADUAL

Ben, a 30-year-old man, told us,

"When my stepdad came into my life, I was like a branch growing one direction for 7 years, and I wish he hadn't tried to rein me back and try to change me so much. I know he loved me, but if a person comes into a relationship involving divorce, there has to be consideration for the way the kids have been raised so far."

Ben went on to tell us the difficult conflicts he faced as he tried to mold himself to both his father's and his stepfather's expectations. They were very different men. It wasn't until Ben reached adulthood that he could actually bring himself to acknowledge that he loved his stepfather. He realizes now that they both contributed important things to his development, but it wasn't easy for him as a child.

A woman in her 30s wrote to us,

"The divorce was rapidly followed by my father's remarriage and the birth of two new children. I learned that change was the only constant thing in my life. I felt betrayed by my father, and my brother suffered even more than I did. I feel parents must communicate with their children. If they can't or won't talk to you, then they should find someone else to talk to about it. Take care of your personal needs but never forget to show your children how much you love them."

Looking back as an adult, she understood that her father had personal needs. Though the adjustment was hard, she didn't feel as hurt by the rapid changes as she did by the lack of communication and relationship with her father. If things have to change quickly, children need to be included and informed. They need to be reassured of their central, safe place in their parents' lives and hearts.

This same sense of feeling rushed and lost in the shuffle is illustrated in this story, shared by a teenage girl:

"When we moved into my stepdad's house, no one asked me if I wanted to, and I hadn't even seen it before. Suddenly, I had this stepbrother who I still don't get along with. I felt so thrown into the situation. My mom pressured me to like him. I still, to this day, don't feel comfortable around him."

DANGERS OF DISCIPLINING

Megan, age 15, offered this bit of wisdom:

"A stepparent doesn't know you like your mom or dad. You aren't theirs, and so that natural thing of love and stuff isn't there. They might overdo it with discipline because they don't have that check inside that would say something like, 'Yeah, that was a rotten thing to do, but this is my kid. . . .' In fact, in some ways, I think heavy-handed stepparents could really be dangerous."

Ryan agreed,

"With normal parents, like moms and dads, they have this sympathy thing, like, 'This is my baby.' But stepparents shouldn't have that much responsibility because they don't have that other side, that this-is-my-baby side. If me and my stepbrother did the same thing wrong, I bet that, not on purpose, my dad would punish him more, and Gloria would punish me more. So stepparents really have to think before they punish."

Ryan's astute observations are born out statistically. Children are much more likely to be physically or sexually abused by a stepparent figure than by their biological parents. Of course, the vast majority of stepparents are loving, caring people who very much want to be a positive force in their stepchildren's lives.

For some, it may be a relief to realize they don't have to become an instant parent. They simply have to begin to get to know and care about their stepchildren. As they do so, it will probably become readily apparent that there are many ways to contribute to a child's positive growth and development without taking on the role of the disciplinarian.

According to our respondents, avoiding the role of disciplinarian altogether is probably the preferred avenue for stepparents. As Tyler, age 12, said,

"Don't allow stepparents to discipline stepchildren."

Stepparenting is a special activity that, at its best, is a blend of mentor, older friend and role model, support system, and guide. If a parent who remarries insists the stepparent assume a disciplinary role, or if the stepparent herself or himself insists, then it is essential that *relationship and trust* come first.

Of course, this does not mean the stepparent just sits by and allows the children to behave in any way they wish. It does not mean the stepparent should be treated disrespectfully. It simply means that the biological parent needs to consistently and directly involved and needs to set the limits and impose the consequences.

"When they start to be like your real parents, and tell you stuff like when you should come home and the way you should be, but still don't trust you the same way your real parents trust you... that pisses me off,"

related Sam, whose mother remarried when he was 15 years old. His stepfather made the deadly mistake of trying to discipline Sam before he had established any kind of trusting, loving relationship.

"It's more like living with a narc or a jailer. I wish he'd back off. He doesn't know me at all."

Wendy, an 18-year-old young woman, told us,

"I went from having no one controlling my life because my dad was working all the time to just make ends meet, and he didn't have time to control me and he trusted me and he used to be my best friend, and then she came along. They got married and she thought that if she governed me that would make my dad happy. She was so controlling, and she still is."

Not only did Wendy feel that her stepmother was given unfair authority, she felt like her stepmother's intentions were not in her best interest, but instead were a means of strengthening her stepmom's ties to her dad.

The age of the children, of course, plays a role in defining the stepparent relationship. Jimmy told us,

"When your parents remarry when you are like in seventh grade you don't need a new mother, so stepparents should just try to be friends, or just be really careful how they gradually phase in rather than just declaring that she's in charge now too."

Kendra, who lived with her mother, observed the following:

"My dad got married to a woman who doesn't like teenagers, so my brother went through a lot of shit with her. I can't imagine living with her."

Doug, a 15-year-old child of divorce and two remarriages, said,

"My stepmom is really nice. She doesn't have any kids. I think that it is hard when stepparents already have kids because my stepdad raised his kids different than my mom raises us, so he will get mad at her sometimes."

Even though Doug reported some conflict between his mom and his stepfather, it is clear that his mother is seen as the one raising her children. Doug's stepfather may disagree, but there are healthy boundaries present in Doug's story. This may account for the empathy he shows in his descriptions. Doug was basically happy with both of his stepparents and with his two-family life in general.

STEPSIBLINGS: BE FAIR, BE WATCHFUL

Tracey, the young woman quoted at the beginning of the chapter, told us,

"When I was little it was okay, but now that I'm older I'm beginning to realize that my stepmother treats her children way better than she treats me. She gives them breaks in their chores and what they eat, so I get stuck with the leftovers."

Besides discipline struggles, the blended family with stepsiblings faces the issue of fairness in some unique ways. Her kids, your kids, my kids, his kids, our kids. As everyone whose ever been a kid remembers, "Unfair!" is the battle-cry between siblings in some pretty rough wars. It is so obvious, it seems silly to stress this, but parents and stepparents must strive to be as fair as they can possibly, humanly be. Of course, absolute fairness is really impossible, but the effort needs to be there.

"My blended family was huge, and totally divided. My step-mom's kids got everything. They had it so much better than us, I couldn't believe it. My dad lives in fear of her, so he just told us to get along. Over and over. She'd cook special stuff for her kids. Do their laundry, but not ours. She'd give them rides and make us walk. And they even got more money than us. I hate her and I hate them."

It may be human nature to favor your own children. It may even occur unconsciously. But it does great harm, and it is worth serious, ongoing consideration.

The same caution offered by Ryan and Megan can be applied to stepsiblings. We heard stories about some pretty mean-spirited older stepsiblings. One such story is included in chapter 7 because of its extreme nature. Parents need to remember that stepsiblings will not necessarily get along naturally. Even the Brady Bunch had trouble occasionally. It is only wise to be on guard for bullying, ganging up, inappropriate sexual behavior, harassment, and other abusive behaviors between stepsiblings.

ANOTHER TIME AROUND

Sometimes, second or even third marriages also end in divorce. In some of these marriages, one of the partners was a stepparent to the other partner's children—sometimes for most of the children's lives. The children and adults we spoke with who had faced multiple divorces strongly believed they wanted the right to stay connected to the ex-stepparent.

> *"My mom hated Michael so much she swore he'd never see us again. And he didn't have any legal rights, so she could do that. And it sucked. My sister and I thought he was pretty cool, but we didn't dare tell Mom that. We missed him."*

Children naturally attach to loving adults in their lives. In fact, they even attach to the not-so-loving adults. These attachments are very important parts of growing up healthy and able to sustain loving adult relationships. As 13-year-old Jay told us,

> *"My parents got divorced when I was 3, and my mom moved us here from Kentucky. So I didn't know my dad very well for years, but Mom remarried this guy named Lenny and he adopted me, and I call him 'Dad' now, and they had my little sister, and then they got divorced, and they would fight and it was hard because the fights were about us. And now I have another dad because my mom is married again. I get attached to people pretty easily, but I try to keep my distance because I don't know if there will be another divorce. I get really scared. I am really glad my sister and I both go see my dad a lot—the one that adopted me."*

Parents need to allow children to have continued contact with people they love and are attached to, whether that be ex-in-laws, ex-stepparents, or even ex-stepgrandparents. Hannah described her loss this way:

> *"My mom and my stepdad got divorced and when I see him on the street, I don't know what to call him. I used to call him 'Dad,' but no one encouraged us to have any sort of relationship after the divorce, even though he was the closest thing I ever had to a father."*

It is also true that children get tired, confused, and guarded after having too many stepparent-type figures come and go in their lives. Shelly, a young mom and child of two divorces, said,

"My mom's on her third marriage after my dad and I'll never open up myself to this current husband. I've dealt with too many of my mom's husbands. I won't allow my kids to call my mother's current husband 'Grandfather' because I don't want them trapped in the same confusion about who to be attached to, like I was with my stepdads."

And Theo, a 17-year-old boy, said,

"My family's divorce was okay. I was too young. I went through another one with my mom and stepdad and that was crazy."

AND NOW FOR SOME GOOD NEWS

Tessa, a well-adjusted and light-hearted 11-year-old girl, said,

"Having divorced parents isn't that bad, it just means twice the birthday presents."

Kids of divorce recognized at many levels that sometimes, good things can come from what initially seems like a very bad or difficult thing. Katy had glowing remarks for her blended family:

"My mom remarried when I was nine and he is a wonderful man. He is so easy going and such a sweetheart. He really has been my dad, even though he never technically adopted us."

Bill, who as an adult, is very thankful for both his father and his stepfather:

"I'm a better person for having been loved by those two guys. My dad was disorganized but good with people. My stepdad helped me get a handle on things. It's one of the good things of divorce."

Tamara's parents divorced when she was very young because her father was an alcoholic and abusive to her mother. She reflected on her experience:

"My dad may have been able to get alcohol treatment and they may have worked things out and marched on together, but thank God they didn't! My stepdad is a nice man who makes a wonderful father."

Darla, a 16-year-old girl, made this comment:

"Both of my parents were remarried when I was 7. I was not al-ways easy on my stepparents, even though I was included in both of the weddings and never felt like I was replaced or ig-nored because of them. As I look back on my life I am very thankful for both of my stepparents. They have given me a broader perspective of ways to deal with the world, as well as two models of how happy, healthy marriages should be. I love both of my families very much."

LaKeisha, a 14-year-old girl, told us that her parents divorced when she was 11. It was an awful time for her. Thankfully, things are much better now, as she shared:

"My parents' divorce was ugly, a necessity, and it sucked. I wish they were still together, but I love my stepparents (they are great). My parents must not have been meant to be together."

Two woman, both in their 40s, told us about only really coming to value their stepparents after they reached adulthood. Betty, whose fa-ther has now been married to her stepmother for 27 years, said,

"I was thinking about the whole thing just the other day. And I thought to myself, 'Good Lord, Dad's been married to Lily over a quarter of a century,' and I had this warm feeling. I realized I really liked her. I should have just gotten the phone and called her. Maybe I still will."

Carol said,

"I've been having some trouble with my own child of divorce, and you know, I called up my mom, and my stepdad got on to say hi. I found myself asking for his advice, and he gave me some very good ideas. He's a good friend. A very good friend. I'm really glad he is in my life."

This poem was written by a gifted young writer who also is clearly keenly tuned into his stepfather's way of being. As the poem illustrates, even though stepparents are not "real" parents, in the sense of biological reproduction, they have very real, lasting, pro-found effects in the lives of their stepchildren.

The Seasons of My Stepfather

Many people say
the eyes are windows to the soul.
Some reveal shifts and changes,
as if they ride the back of the wind
for all to see.

This is true of my stepfather.

His eyes
can hold a lake of frozen ice.
There is death to the steady, rhythmic pulse
of life.

Winter

Moments pass.
The ice gives way to a gentle sea.
Its waters
cradle his fragile craft
of emotions.

Spring

Water slips through hands.
His eyes now burn with fire;
each flame lashes out
to lick bare flesh
and raise the tears and blood
of the innocent.

Summer

Then he is mellow.
We gather around an ancient picture
of his parents.
In the glass
our reflections align with their images
so that the souls of the present
mingle with the ghosts of past.

Fall

SUMMARY

In this chapter, we covered what our respondents had to say about stepparenting. Stepparenting is a unique calling and task. It isn't just like biological parenting, and it isn't just like adopted parenting. Getting the relationship to a positive, healthy place is the first order of business. Taking things slowly and trying to stay out of the role of disciplinarian are both wise moves.

Many children reported that stepparents were a great addition to their lives. That outcome is well worth working for!

CHAPTER 7

Exceptional Cases, Exceptional Needs

This chapter contains advice offered by children who have faced very difficult situations. The sad truth is that some people make choices or have troubles that make them very bad parents. Some parents simply never bother to get involved. Others make grand promises and then repeatedly disappear. Still others have addictions or serious character problems that require extra caution and wisdom on the part of the (hopefully) more adequate parent.

THE TOMB OF THE UNKNOWN PARENT

Sometimes, children grow up only knowing one of their biological parents. In most cases, there seems to be mild to moderate curiosity about the missing parent. Nineteen-year-old Sophie told us,

"My mom left my dad, or vice versa, when I was a baby. I never met him. I knew where he lived, but he never called or anything, and we never tried to reach him. My mom and my half-sister and I made it on our own. But I was always a little curious: What would he be like? I had his last name and I was pretty sure I looked like him, because I didn't look like Mom or my sister at all. So, when I was 17, we moved back to Omaha, and that year, I looked up his phone number and called him. And we got together. At first, it was kind of neat. He seemed to dig getting to know me and stuff. He bought me dinner a couple times. He was married and had three little brats. It wasn't long before he was

I didn't like the guy

asking me to stay at his house on weekends, but all that amounted to was he wanted me to take care of those kids. And he even tried to give me a curfew when I stayed over. Well, that's about it. I know who he is now. Big deal."

For Sophie, and probably for many others, when the unknown parent turns up, it is anything but easy to start any kind of normal relationship. Too much life has passed by. Too many fantasies and too much disappointment are involved; but at least the curiosity is satisfied.

We also talked with a few children and adults who had a very strong feeling that they were just as well off without these unknown parents. Sometimes they believed they knew enough to know this lost parent would be an unsavory person to have in their lives. This is the case with the quote featured on this page. This response was written by a child who was 9 years old. Her parents had divorced when she was 2, and she had not seen her father since. Clearly, her memories of him have been embellished by her own speculations or by information from her mom or other family members. For whatever reasons, she has decided, at least for now, that it is better this way. She never liked the guy anyway.

We also talked with a man whose family seemed to have the ever-popular "don't ask, don't tell" policy. He knew he must have a father, since he was conceived long before sperm donations were available apart from the carrier, but his mother had simply never mentioned the father, and he had simply never asked. He lived in an extended family with his grandparents and had some great male role models in the neighborhood. His own assessment of his life was positive. He is married and functioning happily as a stepfather to two older girls and as a biological father to his son. He admitted that other people might have been more curious about their parentage, but he just never felt the need. His mom is a quiet but strong woman, and her son is very much like her.

These examples are the exception to the rule, but they illustrate an important point. Not all children are curious about or want to actively pursue a relationship with both of their biological parents. Not all children want to know historical family information—even about their own biological origins. It may be a matter of timing, or it may be a matter of temperament, or both. We firmly believe it is the children's right to ask and be told the truth (in developmentally appropriate and sensitive ways). We also firmly believe it is the children's right to choose not to ask, or to declare there are things they do not want to know.

This whole notion gets very tricky, though, because sometimes children do want to know things and don't know how to ask. One 17-year-old girl wrote,

"Parents shouldn't think kids don't care if they don't say something about the other parent. Mostly, they do care, but it is hard to ask."

Parents (and other relatives) need to consider their children's ages, emotional stability, and general temperament before they decide what to say and when. Perhaps an extreme example will help: Telling a 3-year-old child that her mother's drug habit was so bad that her mother left the family to live on the streets is not okay. On the other hand, telling her that her mommy loved her as much as she knew how but was sick and couldn't take care of her is okay, and might be preferable to no mention of mommy at all. As the child grows in maturity, she can be told more of the story if she asks or needs to know.

Custodial parents, when they are the only parent on the scene, need to be sensitive and insightful as they provide their children with information about the missing parent. There are two obvious temptations in this situation. The first is to give the children subtle messages that this is a taboo topic, that they simply should not, under any circumstance, ask for details about their other biological parent. Children may feel very protective of the parent they live with and may not want to upset family members by bringing up uncomfortable topics that seem to cause discomfort. Therefore, they may keep their concerns and needs to know to themselves, and consequently, never have a chance to explore and process their natural curiosity or emotional reactions.

The other temptation is (surprise!) to unload on the children. This is such a ubiquitous and alluring temptation that we have spent many, many pages on this topic in various ways already. But here we are again. It is a truly important message. Just because the other parent is permanently missing, or maybe even dead, you are not free to say whatever you might feel like saying about him or her. It does the child absolutely no good to bear the burden of his or her custodial parent's rage, resentment, hurt, and judgments. Yes, it is okay to tell the child the truth when he or she is emotionally mature enough to handle it. No, it is not okay to add in your own feelings about this truth. To illustrate, read the following two scenarios. Let's say Joe left Mary and their two children, ages 4 and 7. He left for another woman, followed her to another state, and sends money sporadically. Otherwise, he has no contact with the children. Which of Mary's explanations do you think gives each child a better chance at developing into a healthy, happy individual?

Scenario 1

"Mommy, why did daddy leave?"

"Your father left us because he has no morals. He has no sense of commitment. He is a selfish liar, and he hates responsibility. He left with a terrible woman who is just like him. People like your father should have never been born." Mary either throws a dish in the sink and breaks it or bursts into tears.

Scenario 2

"Mommy, why did daddy leave?"

"Why do you ask, honey?"

"'Cause I miss him."

"Yeah, it's hard to have your daddy just disappear, huh?"

"Uh-huh."

"Well, I think he left because he somehow wasn't ready to be a good dad and husband. He probably wanted to be, but right

now, he just couldn't do it. He wanted to be with a different woman, and he moved away. He sends a little bit of money to help us out. It's disappointing and sad sometimes, isn't it? Things don't work out the way we hope, and people don't act the way we want them to sometimes. But I think we'll be okay, don't you? And maybe, someday, your daddy will be in touch and you can get to know him a little bit, anyway."

Many parents ask what to do when children ask hard questions and don't seem to be old enough or stable enough to handle the whole truth. Our answer is this: *Stall, simplify, and soften.* You might think of this as the "3-S solution." Here's an example: Let's say that 4-year-old Billy is being raised by his mom. Billy's dad is in prison for sexual assault. He overhears family conversation and asks his mom, "Mommy, what is sexual salt?"

A good answer would begin with an inquiry. This clarifies what the child really wants to know, and why. Often, it helps stall things a little too, so the adult has time to think of how to handle the situation. One answer might be, "That's quite a grown-up question, son. Tell me why you want to know." We can assume Billy would say something like, "Well, I heard Aunt Josie say that was what my dad did." But sometimes children say something that tells you about their needs—something that otherwise, you might have missed. Billy could answer, "Well, at preschool, I heard the teacher say it and she said it was something nasty. Is it?"

This calls for a much different answer. The first response indicates a direct question about his dad, and both issues need to be addressed, for example, "Billy, sexual assault is something that isn't nice. It is a grown-up problem. Your daddy did something that was not nice and he got in trouble for it. When you get older, we can talk some more about it, okay?" To the second, more general question, the answer can be more general. "Yes, Billy, sexual assault isn't nice. It is usually a grown-up problem, though. It means when someone touches someone else in a way that they don't want to be touched. We'll read a book about touching pretty soon. Maybe when you're five. And then we can talk some more about this. Okay?" Depending on Billy's needs, language development, and environment, this conversation may go on for a little while, or the brief exchange in the example above may be enough for now.

Never shoot from the hip when something as complicated as explaining parental betrayal, criminal behavior, abandonment, or death. It is fine to tell inquiring children that their question is very important, and you need to think about your answer for a while before the two of you talk. It is a good idea to consult with friends, family, or even professionals about the best way to tell a child a difficult truth. It will usually be an incremental process, spread out over the years of your relationship with your children.

A 6-year-old boy whose father was in prison told us,

"I wish that my mom could make my dad come home, and she said that she would if she could. He lives far, far away."

This mom is making a hard choice about how much to tell and when. She has no way of knowing if her child's father will ever make contact with them again, and for now, she has decided the child only needs to know that his father is far away.

PARTIAL ABANDONMENT

"My parents got divorced when I was three, and my mom turned gay when she left my dad. My dad got custody, and my mom would come pick me up to take me to the park or something, and she always told me she was going to get me stuff, and she'd say all these things she was going to do for me, and then she'd disappear for like 2 years. I got to the point that I hated her. I didn't even want her to talk to me because it was all lies. Like she said if I got good grades, she'd help with my car insurance. Two years, not a dime. Last Christmas, I didn't even hear from her. Or Easter. In fact, I graduated from high school and I didn't hear a thing from my mom, or from her mom either. I sent them both announcements. Not even a card or anything. I would rather not have had her in my life at all than to have her in my life and treat me like that. From my mother, I learned how to shut down and never look back. Because of her, I can just shut people off. That sucks. I kind of look down on gay women because of her and her friends. I'm sure there are nice gay people in the real world, though."

This 18-year-old woman is clearly still experiencing pain and confusion from the sporadic, dishonest relationship her mother offered her. She is mature enough to realize that all lesbians would not treat their children the same way, but it is hard to carry all that failure and not project some hatred toward the group her mother joined, or the identity her mother developed.

Ted, a graduate student in his 20s, told us the following story:

"My mom filed for divorce when I was 2, and afterwards, I only saw my biological father a few times a year. What little time I spent with him was usually devoted to him playing poker with his buddies. I don't think he really knew how to spend time with me.

When I was about 10, my mom married Ed. For the first time in my life, I began to understand what it really meant to have a father. Ed played basketball with me, taught me to shoot a gun, and took me skiing and camping. We did a lot of family things. I was included in everything.

A year or so after they married, I asked my mom and Ed if I could have the same last name as they did. It was my own idea. I wanted Ed to adopt me. My parents filed for adoption, and heard no response, so they thought the court visit would just be a formality. But no, there was my biological father, Tom, and his father, and an attorney. Tom took the stand and said I was his son and no one else's, and he even flashed me a victory sign. That made me mad. Tom never even asked me what I wanted. He made me feel like a piece of property, not a real person with needs or feelings of my own.

Later that day, I had to tell the judge, in private, that I did not love Tom. I told the judge that Ed was more of a father to me. I knew what I wanted, but that was really hard. That impression stuck with me for many years.

The adoption was awarded. For years, I was so mad at Tom that I refused to talk to him on the phone. One time, some years later, in Tom's presence, I referred to Ed as 'my dad' and Tom got very angry with me. So I stopped doing that, but the fact is, Ed is my dad. And now, almost 20 years later, Tom and I have a very tenuous relationship. He is a distant friend. I still don't call him 'father.'

I know that a divorce was the best thing for my mother and Tom. I don't regret the split at all. What I do resent is that one of my parents forgot to consider my wants and feelings. From my perspective, Tom wanted me to be his son as long as it didn't require any work or money from him. He wanted me to have his name, but he didn't want to spend time with me or be a father to me. If Tom had simply talked to me, listened to me, and respected me, we might have a much closer relationship than I think we will ever have now."

In most cases, our respondents seemed to feel that a little contact with their biological parents was better than none. Nevertheless, they were also clear that the in-and-out nature of this contact takes a serious toll on them, and it does not build a true parent-child relationship. At best, it keeps the parent from being a complete stranger. At worst, it sets the child up for disappointment over and over again. Each contact holds the promise of more—the promise of a relationship, the promise of support, the promise of love. But the repeated disappearances, the failed promises, and the dashed hopes grow increasingly hard to bear. Simply being the biological sperm or egg donor does not give biological parents an instant or permanent parent-child bond.

The parent with whom children live cannot completely protect the children from the pain of this partial abandonment, but respondents who had had to cope with this scenario often expressed deep gratitude to the stable parent in their lives. One 15-year-old girl told us the following:

"My dad makes me promises about things. Then he disappears. And I know this, but I keep thinking he'll change. Like, he said he'd get me a kennel for my dog, and I wanted a kennel really bad. My mom knew I'd never see that kennel. She said she'd try to buy one, but it wasn't just the kennel. I wanted my dad to keep a promise, so I said no to my mom. And she understood, I think. I never did get a kennel. I finally got an old dog house from a neighbor."

SERIOUS PATHOLOGY AND ENDANGERMENT

Another exceptional situation involves one or both parents being dangerous, unfit parents, providing unsafe environments for the children. The following is an excerpted story, shared with us by Rod, a young man from the Midwest:

"My mother was always very careful not to badmouth my father. As much as he had harmed and continued to harm her through emotional abuse and manipulation, she would not speak ill of him. This, of course, sounds like a wonderful principle. However, the reality is my father suffers from serious character pathology and a number of addictions. My mother may have not had the technical skill to label his pathologies, but she did know how damaging he was. Because she refused to say anything negative about him (he did not return the courtesy), I grew up assuming that the difficulty I had relating to him and understanding him was some intrinsic flaw in myself.

Furthermore, as my mother tried to respect my father, she made no careful inquiries about what he did with us and what environment he exposed us to during our yearly vacation together, or on the Saturdays we were expected to be at his house. He needed to be challenged, and wasn't. As a result, my siblings and I were exposed to reams of pornography, drug use, and excessive drinking. He would drive us down to Missouri from Wisconsin every summer. As he drove, we popped beers for him and mixed his drinks. I could mix a whiskey sour by the time I was six, and bested my siblings in the popularity contest this way. By the time we hit the Missouri border, he was forging into oncoming traffic to pass cars in no-passing zones. He made it seem like a fun game, throwing imaginary grenades out the window at the person he passed, laughing and screaming, 'Die, lady, die!' It didn't dawn on me until I was grown that this was absurd, dangerous, and illegal behavior. To me, it was normal.

Don't let your desire to respect your ex, or your desire to avoid dealing with her or him, interfere with your judgment about the safety of your children. Do not let your silence about the other parent be so complete that the children cannot make sense out of their struggle to relate to a difficult, limited, or mean person."

The majority of parents who want to stay involved in their children's upbringing are neither saint nor devil, neither perfect nor fatally flawed. Many, if not most, are irritating sometimes, irresponsible once in a while, and exercise poor judgment on occasion. Opportunities arise to be critical of almost anyone's parenting practices. Refraining from doing so is the challenge presented in the bulk of this book. However, Rod's story speaks to an entirely different level of concern. Children in the care of a dangerous parent need to be listened to, and protective action needs to be taken.

Any parent who detests the other parent is prone to exaggerate the bad traits and potential dangers of the other. Consultation with an unbiased third party might be necessary to determine if the children are actually in danger of being harmed physically or psychologically by the behavior of the other parent. Children can tolerate quite a bit of oddity. They can weather inconsistencies, varieties of discipline strategies, disappointments, and worries. These things aren't ideal by any means, but it also isn't the same thing as real endangerment. Learning to adjust to our parents' imperfections is part of life for all of us.

An important source of ongoing information about how time with the other parent is going is the children themselves. Jason, age 17, told us about the fear that kept him from ever telling his mother about his father's use of physical punishment, some of which was quite abusive:

"I knew if I told anyone, it would just cause a big blow up. It wasn't worth it. She wanted to get him back for so many things, she would have used it instead of helping me sort it out."

Without a doubt, children do *not* want to be quizzed about their time at the other parent's house, but kind, nonjudgmental inquiry is different than being grilled. Children need to feel sure that they can discuss cruel, scary, sexual, or other inappropriate behavior they are subjected to by any other human being—which includes parents and other relatives. The safety to do so comes, in part, by parents behaving in respectful ways toward their ex-spouse. If the child does not feel pumped for bad information, if the child does not feel anything said will be used vindictively toward the other parent, if the child feels there is a commitment to honesty and fairness, then the chances for disclosure of concern about other parent's behaviors are much, much higher.

As we mentioned in chapter 6, stepsiblings require extra parental attention. When there is little trust between the parent and the children, and children have no one in whom they can confide, the situation can truly be dangerous. This traumatic story was told to us by Kim, a 17-year-old girl who was 6 at the time of her parents' divorce:

"My dad got involved right away with a woman who had a slightly older son. I spent most of my time at my dad's, and I fought all the time with her son. He loved beating me up. I tried to fight back, and I never told anyone. Once, he broke a bone in my foot, and another time, he broke my arm. Both times, I had to go to the hospital. But nobody asked much about it. Mom was trying to get her shit together, getting into her own life, and she didn't spend that much time with me. When she did spend time, I didn't want to complain. And I was scared to complain to dad very much. He was having enough trouble with the relationship. I didn't know if I would even be allowed to stay. I was terrorized for years."

Rachel, a young woman in her 20s, told us,

"I was 11 when my parents divorced. They got divorced because my dad was an alcoholic. Once, he almost burned the house down because he fell asleep while he was frying something. My mom said, 'That's it, we're leaving.' I was so glad. I was scared of him. They fought a lot. We had to do weekends with my dad. I didn't like that. He'd get drunk and cry and badmouth my mom. I'd have to call and get my mom to come pick me up. When I was in eighth grade my mom married another alcoholic. Growing up, I had a horrible model of what marriage should be, so I grew up, got married, and got divorced. I really try, when my child has questions about his dad, to just let him know why he can't see his dad. I don't badmouth him or say things that aren't true so that my child won't have to grow up with what I had to grow up with."

This young mother's struggles to find a better way to raise her son were inspiring to hear. She was determined to be protective and honest. Finding a way to tell children about the failings of their other parent without sounding vindictive or judgmental is a difficult but important gift.

DON'T "FAKE GOOD" FOR THE OTHER PARENT

Perhaps attempting to give children a positive view of the world, some parents choose to pretend the other parent was or is a fine person. Our interview participants were clear on this as well. Mario, a middle-aged man, shared,

> *"My advice to any parent going through a divorce is to try and be as honest as possible with your children. In my case my mother painted a false positive picture of my dad. She thought she was doing the best for us at the time and maybe she was, but now that I'm older I've come to realize my father is not who I thought he was. And it is very difficult right now. My mom did everything for us and my father, nothing. But my mom passed everything off as both of their doing."*

The story from Rod earlier in this chapter also underlines the importance of this honesty. He feels, to this day, that his mother's false "respect" for his father not only left him and his siblings unsafe, it confused them as to who really had the problems. Children expect their parents to be basically good people. When their relationships with their parents are going all wrong, they tend to look inward and blame themselves, especially when they are young.

Again, we want to stress that there are ways to acknowledge the other parent's dysfunction without judging or condemning them. For example, 16 year-old Carey, who wrote the following poem, was coping with a suicidal father. The poem recounts how she tried to stand for life in the face of her father's despair. It is a beautiful poem, but tragic. Children should never be asked to stand where this young poet has stood. But it would not help Carey to hear that her father is a self-pitying, lying drunk. Instead, her mother needs to help protect her and needs to limit the times and ways Carey and her father spend time together. Carey's mother can say (many times and in many ways), "Carey, your father is depressed. He's abusing alcohol and he's not making good choices about his life right now. It isn't your fault and neither of us can fix him. He has to find his own way."

Skeletons

Tears fought from falling taste
salty in the back of your throat
as you remember Mom, back in '78.
What seemed to be the beginning
of a twenty year heaven

But leaves dried and crumbled
just as your heart. You want to escape
but there ain't a place that far.

Mom shouldn't have judged
a book by its cover.
You've lied to her and me for too long.

Now loneliness clouds your thoughts.
Guns, large explosives, drugs
sing sweet songs in your head.

You say you'd like to blow up something
the post office by the Masonic Temple,
to end your pain in a mushroom cloud.

I fall deeper into the wormhole,
traveling further into fear. Your little Bug Bug
squashed between the two of you
knowing too much and confused as hell.

Are your friends as high as you
thinking it's okay
to lie and cheat a family.

Papa, je t'aime!
Don't end it all now.
Please think of how things could be,
grandchildren, a great estate...

May tomorrow be the reason
Today isn't a good day
to die.

SUMMARY

This chapter covered the less usual and more difficult situations some divorcing parents face, including abandonment, repeated failures to keep promises or contact, and serious pathology or endangerment. Parents and children facing these situations deserve special support and understanding.

Every situation described in this chapter calls for extraordinary wisdom, maturity, and strength on the part of the parent who is trying to cope with an absent or seriously dysfunctional co-parent. Not only must they face most of the parenting tasks alone, but they must also find ways to acknowledge the other parent's shortcomings and failings without condemning them to the children. We feel strongly that such parents deserve all the support and assistance they can find. Therefore, we want to encourage you, if this is what you face, to seek professional help, family support, community and church support, and to strive to take care of yourself.

CHAPTER 8

Resources for Divorcing Families

Hundreds of children of divorce contributed their thoughts, feelings, and advice to this book. We've tried to faithfully reflect their words and experiences. But remember, these messages weren't really offered to us—they were offered to you, members of families facing divorce. Obviously, the messages and advice and stories come from the particular lives and experiences of each child, so the specifics may not apply to every parent. But taken together, the chorus is strong and the message is clear. As families divorce, children need their parents to stay deeply committed to them and their well-being. This chapter shifts gears a bit in an attempt to help you identify the resources you will need to follow the children's advice.

USE THIS BOOK!

This book is a resource for you to use with your children. You can use it to talk with them about any feelings they might have concerning divorce. You can read parts or all of it to them, or have them read it and then talk about the different opinions and concerns raised. Hearing what other children have said may free your children to speak up for themselves. You could even invite them to write their own advice, or to write a poem or draw a picture. Of course, when you use resources like this book, do so gently, interactively, and with a spirit of interest and curiosity. If you give your child this book and insist that the two of you have a meeting to formally discuss it at a specific time, you may find that your child will put up strong resistance. In other words, don't use the battering ram approach to parent-child communication.

A social worker friend of ours is always reminding us that, when it comes to getting children to talk, the door locks from the inside. Children are in control of what they choose to say to us and what they choose not to say to us. Our best option is to knock on the door gently and respectfully, to let the children know how interested we are in hearing their perspective.

As you go through your divorce experience, you may need to latch on to any reasonable method you can find to enhance open communication between you and your child. Let them know you are an adult—you can withstand their anger, understand their pain, and be there for them. And remember, don't ask them to be there for you or to take care of your needs.

GETTING THE GOODS

Our choices about resources described in this chapter were guided by the content of the children's advice. It isn't easy to hear words that are blunt and sometimes disturbing—and it is especially hard if you feel you have no idea how to enact what is being requested. The following divorce-related resources can help give you the strength, support, and wisdom you will need to implement some of the children's advice.

SELECTING PROFESSIONAL RESOURCES

Many divorce education resources directed toward both children and adults exist. Some of these resources are available nationally or internationally, whereas others are designed for local communities. If you naively visit a big bookstore thinking you'll just pick up a little something on divorce, here's a word to the wise: Prepare to be overwhelmed. There are literally hundreds, if not thousands, of books, videotapes, audiotapes, CD-ROMs, support groups, classes, and Internet sites designed to provide divorce education to adults and children. Unfortunately, due to the overwhelming number of divorce education programs available in the United States, our review of nationally based resources is not comprehensive. The ones we've described are popular, credible, and likely to be shown effective in future years. Since we cannot possibly review even all the good resources, we encourage you to venture out there and look over some of your options.

Not all of the resources available are worth buying. There are many versions of snake oil and many reincarnations of the master charlatan. Some professionals and organizations are out to make a quick buck; they are more concerned about getting your money than they are in providing you with up-to-date, useful information. To avoid buying poor quality materials, remember these points:

- Make phone calls, ask questions, and get direct advice from people you trust or recognized authorities about the quality of the product you are thinking about purchasing.
- Evaluate the price. Because they are partially funded by city, county, and state funds, many local programs are priced much more reasonably than national programs; it is not always necessary to pay more to get high-quality resources.
- Check the credentials of the producers or authors. Look for some evidence that they've studied the field.
- Scan the materials to make sure they represent your own core values and don't seem too obtuse or simplistic.

DIVORCE RESOURCES FOR KIDS

As demonstrated throughout the first seven chapters of this book, children have wide-ranging reactions to divorce. The specific reactions of each child are based on temperament, age, sex, maturity, and his or her unique relationships with each family member. Every child is different, and every family situation is unique. Therefore, when exploring divorce resources for kids, beware of programs that give you the one-size-fits-all message. The information that follows will help you find resources that fit your individual and family needs.

Children of Divorce Classes

When you're deciding whether to enroll your child in a class designed to help with children's adjustment to divorce, ask questions about the format and content of the class. Basic classes for children should (a) be facilitated by a licensed or certified professional; (b) include children of similar ages in the same class (i.e., there should be separate classes for 6–8 year-olds and 9–12 year-olds); (c) include content pertaining to identifying, understanding, and expressing difficult emotions, dealing with stressed-out parents, communication skills training, and opportunities for group discussion and personal expression; and (d) include resources for parents.

Numerous children of divorce class curricula are available in the U.S. Two of the most prominent classes are the Rollercoasters program and the Sandcastles program. Each program provides children with educational opportunities, chances to see that other children are experiencing difficult times associated with divorce, and activities that promote self-expression.

Rollercoasters	The Sandcastles Program
Families First	M. Gary Neuman, LMHC
1105 Peachtree St., N.E.	P.O. Box 40291
P.O. Box 7948, Station C	Miami Beach, FL 33140-0691
Atlanta, GA 30357-0948	Web site:
Web site: www.familiesfirst.org	www.sandcastlesprogram.com

If you enroll your child in a divorce education class, keep the following information in mind:

- Initially, depending upon his or her age and personality, your child will probably not be eager to participate in a divorce class (you may need to provide your child with an incentive, like a new t-shirt or some other treat, for attending the class).
- Do not expect your child to come home from the class with all of his or her anxiety about divorce instantly resolved. Sometimes the class may, at first, increase your child's anxiety about divorce; this often happens when people are encouraged to talk about things that are hurting them or that they have been avoiding.

- Do not expect your child to eagerly report to you everything that he or she learned in the class. Children may be quiet and thoughtful after attending their class, so you might want to do something quiet or fun and avoid intense discussions.
- Do not expect that attending one series of classes will resolve your child's emotional or behavioral reactions to divorce. Adjustment to divorce is a long-term process that may take many years, many discussions, and even many classes.

Divorce Books and Games for Children and Families

Divorce books and games are sometimes used within the context of a divorce class for children. You can also use these books and games yourself, as you try to communicate with your child about his or her thoughts and feelings about divorce.

The most popular divorce education book for young children is probably the modern classic *Dinosaurs Divorce*, by Lorena and Marc Brown. This book is generally well regarded by both parents and professionals. It is primarily for elementary school-age children, but can be read aloud to preschoolers and may be interesting to some slightly older children. The book consists of 30 color pages that discuss a wide range of divorce-related issues, including parental arguments and potential remarriage. Usually, the ideal purpose of a book like this one is to stimulate parent-child discussion. So, when it comes to having your child read the book, do not use the old shy-parent approach to sex education, which involves dropping a book on his or her bed or leaving it on the kitchen table for him or her to accidentally discover. Instead, use the book to create opportunities for parent-child interaction or discussion about divorce. A word of caution, however: Don't force your children to talk about divorce. Be persistent, open, and watchful. Your children might be ready to talk at the strangest of times. If possible, drop everything and talk then. The ideal situation is for divorce discussions to occur more naturally, because children of all ages frequently react negatively to the experience of being interrogated by their parents.

A book like *Dinosaurs Divorce* can also help children feel more normal about their very personal reactions to divorce. Although the book was rated very high in a fairly recent survey of mental health professionals, it is by no means the only divorce education book available for elementary school-age children. As a rule, because of different family tastes and family values, we recommend that you take time to evaluate different books that might be most appropriate for use with your child or children.

A divorce book that could be read by almost anyone in a family system going through a divorce is Jill Krementz's *How It Feels When Parents Divorce.* This book was published in 1996 and includes the divorce stories of children ages 7 through 17, told in their own words. It is not intended to provide direct advice, but serves to normalize the divorce experience for families who are going through it. The stories include very difficult experiences as well as happy ones and provide a glimpse into each specific child's emotional reactions and thoughts. The book, complete with pictures of each child, is interesting, easy reading and would offer comfort to most children who read it.

Another book written for divorcing families, specifically for adolescents, is *When Divorce Hits Home,* by Beth Joselow and Thea Joselow. This book includes many excellent tips for teenagers whose parents are divorcing. It includes firsthand accounts from teens who have experienced divorce. The authors open their book by stating, "This is not a book for people who are getting divorced. This is not a book for the lawyers, friends, or pets of people who are getting divorced. This is a book for the children of people who are getting divorced." If there is a flaw at all in this book, it might be that it tends to place too much of the divorce adjustment burden on the children. Therefore, it would be best if both parents and teens read the book and discuss it. Even though it wasn't the authors' stated intent, it has some great material for parents, so it could certainly be considered as a parent resource as well.

DIVORCE RESOURCES FOR PARENTS

Parenting Classes for Divorced or Divorcing Adults

Across the United States, there are many classes for divorcing parents. In some states, couples with children will not be granted a divorce unless they have completed a divorce education class. Some of you reading this book may not have a choice about attending a divorce class and, depending on the size of your community, you may not have a choice over which class you take. (In small communities there may be only one divorce class available.)

Sometimes, parents who are required to take a divorce class are sick and tired of the divorce process and deeply resent being forced to take a class by court mandate. If this is the case for you, we recommend a minor attitude adjustment: When you go to the class, go because you want to learn as much as possible for your children's sake. This small attitude change makes all the difference in how you will feel about the class and how helpful it can be for you. The essay below gives you a glimpse of what it might be like to enroll in a divorce class that has both mandatory and voluntary participants.

Divorce Classes for Parents: An Insider's Look

I'm sitting knee to knee in a circle with 10 other men and women. No one really wants to be here. It's a sunny Saturday morning. I was hoping for rain; Saturday classes that last 6 hours are much easier when it's raining.

Class is about to start. I offer food, but no one eats. A few people slip into the kitchen and fill their cups with coffee or tea. On the opposite side of the circle, a big and sort of burly guy in his mid-30s stares into space. He looks angry and so, for now, I avoid eye contact. Instead, I make small talk. My chatter includes how the local men's and women's sports teams have been doing, the short- and long-term weather forecast, and other conflict-free topics. I make a point of not bringing up religion, politics, or recent changes in child custody law.

During introductions the burly man puts his head in his hands and starts to cry. The room is quiet as he talks about missing his son and daughter. Two other parents silently wipe away tears. Only 15 minutes have gone by and these parents are already deeply into their emotional pain. Suddenly there are no more involuntary participants in this class; everyone in the room is just a parent—a sad, frustrated, and angry parent missing their children and hating part-time parenting.

continues

(continued)

Divorce is an unnatural state. Children become emotionally attached to their parents and then are required to spend extended time periods separated from one parent or another. Obviously, this is difficult and emotionally painful for children and parents. Sometimes people react to the fact that divorce can have negative effects on children by claiming that society should make it harder for parents to divorce. Although this is a tempting solution, research on children of divorce generally indicates that it is not the divorce itself that is most profound in producing negative emotions and behaviors; instead, it is exposure to conflict, hostility, and abuse occurring within families and between estranged or divorced parents that primarily contributes to children's maladjustment.

Parents who are divorced, considering divorce, or from highly conflict-ridden families should educate themselves regarding how to minimize damage to their children. One part of this education may include enrolling in and completing a divorce education class. If you enroll in a divorce education class, try to keep a positive and open attitude. You may be surprised by what you experience.

In the end, the class that, in the beginning, wouldn't eat, wants to order pizza together. Every participant has found they share a common passion. Parents come to this class because they love their children. To be better parents despite the challenge of divorce is their common goal. They leave the building knowing that they are not alone in their pain and struggles. They leave with renewed resolve to protect their children from the trauma of divorce.

Books for Parents

Books that are designed to be read by parents come in all shapes and sizes. Main categories include the following:

- Books about divorce and shared parenting
- Books about how children respond to divorce
- Books about dealing with very difficult ex-spouses
- Books about legal aspects of divorce

In our opinion, the second edition of Isolina Ricci's groundbreaking book, *Mom's House, Dad's House: Making Shared Custody Work* tops the list of books about divorce and shared parenting. Dr. Ricci is firm and balanced in her approach to helping parents shift from their previous romantic relationship to a new business relationship (wherein the business is child-rearing!). This book also provides excellent advice on how to develop parenting plans, and includes a sample parenting plan.

If you're curious about how children respond to divorce and want detailed information on how to talk with your child about divorce and divorce issues, M. Gary Neuman's book, *Helping Your Kids Cope With Divorce: The Sandcastles Way* is a good choice. This book includes chapters on children's play and art, how children of different ages respond to divorce differently, and lots of children's drawings and poetry. Our only complaint about this book is that it uses the outdated language of custody and visitation rather than the more appropriate language of shared or co-parenting. Nonetheless, Neuman's book will give parents great insights into the struggles faced by children of divorce.

When we teach divorce classes for parents, we usually take some time to show parents different books they might want to purchase or check out from their local library. For parents involved in high-conflict divorces, the typical book of choice—and the one that receives the most moans and cheers—is titled *Joint Custody With a Jerk*. Not surprisingly, the title of this book, written by Julie Ross and Judy Corcoran, resonates with how many divorcing parents have come to feel about their former spouse. The book provides helpful tips to parents who are experiencing a high-conflict divorce situation, but you should not let your children or your former spouse see that you own this book. The title, in that context, is quite inflammatory.

For gay or lesbian parents, there are many wonderful resources. Among them are April Martin's book, *The Lesbian and Gay Parenting Handbook*, and *Families of Value: Gay and Lesbian Parents and Their Children Speak Out* by Jane Drucker. Also, the Internet can be a source of support and information for all sorts of parenting challenges.

STRESS MANAGEMENT IDEAS FOR PARENTS

For this final portion of the book, we are switching hats, and drawing from our current work with parents who are divorcing. During a typical week, we get many calls from divorced or divorcing parents in distress. Some examples include:

- A 14 year-old girl who refuses to spend time with her father during "his" weekends. She claims he is "too controlling" and insists that he stop calling her when she is staying at her mother's house.
- A 6 year-old boy whose parents just separated and who is sobbing and clinging to his mother when she tries to drop him off at his father's house. In an interesting development, when the boy is asked how he feels about the divorce, he forcefully insists that he isn't getting to see his father enough.
- A first-time father who called and asked if he can take his 15-month-old son swimming with him at a local pool. He is worried that if he makes any parenting mistakes that his son's mother will take his son away from him.
- A mother who called to complain of her 4-year-old daughter's bizarre behavior during bath time. She fears that her daughter has been sexually abused.
- A concerned mother who wonders, "How old should children be when they are left alone to fend for themselves?" After further conversation, she reveals that her 11-year-old son is home alone at his father's house. She is angry because she cannot force her son's father to call her or hire a babysitter when he goes out.

There's no doubt about it: Divorce is stressful! Each of the preceding scenarios includes a very distressed parent. As a divorced parent, sometimes you will get stressed out about seemingly simple situations (like the man who is worried about taking his 15-month-old child swimming). Other times you will feel upset about potentially very serious matters (such as possible physical or sexual abuse of your children). For a moment, consider the following question: What do you believe is the most important thing you can do to contribute to your child's mental and emotional health?

Parents respond to that question in a variety of ways: consistency, discipline, love, good communication. Each of these responses reflects something very significant that parents can provide for their children. Each aspect is very important to your children's mental and emotional health. But based on what children have told us in preceding chapters, perhaps the most important thing you can provide your children is your *own* mental and emotional health. If you don't tend to your own mental and emotional health, you won't be in much of a position to parent your children well.

We think that the mental and emotional health of parents is so important that we have devoted the remainder of this book to the topic. Our discussion of stress management for parents includes three main topics: preparing for stress, becoming aware of stress, and coping with stress.

Preparing for Stress

You've probably heard the old saying, currently heard primarily from insurance salespeople: If you fail to plan, you're planning to fail. We reiterate this statement here because we're interested in selling you a particular type of psychological insurance. We call this "stress management insurance."

Another relevant old saying is: Knowledge is power. At the core, even if you can't predict what types of stresses or challenges you will face in the years to come, you do know that you will face stress. Plan on it . . . and plan for it.

Cultivate a Support System for Your Children. The first stress management rule for divorcing parents is probably the most important. You can't do it all yourself. You can't be your child's mother, father, companion, confidant, and provider, while simultaneously having any life of your own. When we talk with parents about stress management, the biggest complaint we usually hear is, "I don't have time to manage my stress!" Our response is. . . the McDonald's principle.

The McDonald's principle does not mean that you should eat lots of fast foods. Instead, like the 1970s McDonald's ad campaign, remember that you do "deserve a break today." Divorced parents must take breaks; you must figure out ways to live a balanced and healthy lifestyle. And, to take breaks, you need to cultivate a safe and comfortable support system for your children.

Research on child development indicates that children are mentally and emotionally more healthy when they have close relationships with loving, kind people outside of their nuclear family. The reason this is particularly important for divorcing families is that the pain of divorce doesn't just hit the children, it hits the parents as well. Consequently, you will not always be at your best. In fact, you may find yourself feeling lousy and behaving in ways that you hate. If you're feeling and acting miserable, your children may be well served by spending time with their grandparents, aunt, uncle, or some other kind and trustworthy adult.

The fact is, children can develop attachments to several adults at once. Although young children might prefer to spend all of their time with their mother or father, they can also learn that other adults are safe, interesting, and fun. As a parent, you can select a few friends, relatives, and neighbors and directly ask them about forming meaningful relationships with your children. These additional attachments will pay off—big time—for both you and your child.

Becoming Aware of Stress

Everybody has their own unique way of responding to stress. Some people get angry, active, and competitive. Others feel sharp pains in their stomach, become overwhelmed, or act passive. The first step to effective stress management is to become more aware of what kinds of things are stressful to you and how you react to stress.

Physical Stress Reactions. Physical reactions to stress are fairly easy to spot and are often so distressing to people that the symptoms of stress add to the stress. You might find yourself experiencing any of the following physical symptoms: skin rashes, ulcers, headaches, hair loss, fatigue, loss of appetite, insomnia, shortness of breath, sore shoulders or other sore muscles, and high blood pressure, just to name a few.

Due to the influence of genetic factors in determining physical health and illness, it can be especially important for you to analyze your own physical vulnerabilities to stress. You can do this in two simple ways. First, the next time you are exposed to a difficult and stressful situation, take an inventory of your bodily reactions. Ask yourself: "Where, in my body, am I feeling the stress?" Then, depending on the bodily locations in which you find yourself accumulating stress, you can begin taking steps to address or reduce your physical reaction.

Second, it can be informative for you to take a quick family history of physical ailments. For example, you may discover that your family has a history of migraines, high blood pressure, or ulcers. Again, with this information in hand, you can then construct yourself a stress management plan that will address your personal vulnerabilities.

Physical Coping Responses. Generally speaking, when you are suffering from physical distress, it makes sense to seek a physical solution. Your first, and possibly best, option for coping with physical distress is physical exercise. Many people hate to exercise, but the fact remains that engaging in regular aerobic exercise is an incredibly effective way to reduce physical distress. Additionally, weight lifting and stretching routines (such as yoga) are also very effective in helping people cope with and manage stress.

Other basic physical approaches to stress management include these:

- Establishing and maintaining a healthy diet that includes plenty of fruits and vegetables
- Learning and regularly applying physical relaxation techniques such as deep breathing or progressive muscle relaxation
- Avoiding or minimizing alcohol consumption and drug use

Sometimes parents who are experiencing divorce complain about the "cod liver oil" phenomenon. Essentially, this means that parents are feeling frustrated because everything that is "good for them" tastes bad, while everything that is "bad for them" tastes good. If only chocolate was naturally packed with vitamins, minerals, and fiber. Well, the stark reality is that healthy habits often require vast amounts of self-discipline and willpower. And the foundation to developing these habits is a healthy attitude.

Mental Reactions to Stress. Stress can get into your brain. The results can include decreased concentration, trouble making decisions, repetitive negative thoughts about yourself and your life situation, difficulty solving conflicts and problems because of an inability to perceive positive alternatives or options, and systematic distortions of reality.

One of the most common mental reactions to stress is discouragement or pessimism. It can seem as if everything is going wrong, and soon you may expect more of the same negative occurrences from moment to moment. This type of negative mindset can be extremely draining, and to counter it you will need encouragement and support.

Another common mental reaction to stress is polarized thinking. Polarized thinking occurs when you have extreme and dichotomous reactions to situations, such as thinking that something that happens is either terrible or wonderful. When polarized thinking takes over, it is hard to consider any middle ground about issues. It gets harder and harder to view life's ups and downs from the proper perspective. Even worse, polarized thinking can eventually affect your ability to come up with reasonable solutions to life's daily problems. For example, when your daughter's father arrives late to pick her up for soccer practice, you may see your only options as either yelling something totally crude at him or playing martyr and staying quiet about the whole situation.

Mental Coping Responses. Usually, the physical coping responses listed above can have a positive effect on mental stress. In many cases, physical exercise can help you "blow off steam," and then you will be able to think more constructively and hopefully about whatever problem you're facing.

There are also numerous mental approaches to stress management. Perhaps the most popular and straightforward approach to settling your mind is meditation. Unfortunately, meditation can be difficult, especially for people who are experiencing high stress levels. Many people who try to meditate find that initially, they feel more anxious and upset than ever. Therefore, if you're interested in meditation, enroll in a meditation class or follow specific procedures outlined in a meditation book.

Another way to tackle mental stress is to actually work on changing the way you think about things. You might think of this as a positive attitude adjustment, but to really change the way you think takes hard work and dedication. If you're interested in making mental changes, you may want to track down one of the many books that have been written to guide people in making cognitive changes to reduce stress, depression, and anxiety. You may also want to consider professional counseling.

Social Reactions to Stress. Some people find that going through a divorce causes such a sense of loss or shame that they simply don't want to venture out and see people. This can result in social isolation, which has been shown to contribute further to stress and illness. Consequently, during the especially difficult time of divorce, it turns out that parents frequently add to their own burden and vulnerability by isolating themselves.

Social Coping Responses. The Girl Scout song that says, "Make new friends, but keep the old. One is silver and the other gold," should be something you sing to yourself every morning. Seriously. Helpful and healthy social relationships lead to better physical health and more adaptive coping strategies. So do what you can to counter your impulses to completely hibernate and avoid everyone. Develop your social support system and talk as openly as possible with people you trust.

The fact that social isolation is a negative way to react to stressful situations doesn't mean that divorcing parents should avoid spending time alone. Taking a personal retreat, being by yourself from time to time, and getting away from the daily grind can all be positive coping responses.

Emotional Reactions to Stress. As we noted previously, in the face of stress, some people get angry, and others may feel fear, sadness, guilt, or disgust. We recommend that you take time to analyze your usual emotional response to stress. That way you can be more prepared to cope with the emotions that will well up inside during stressful times in your life.

Strong emotions can be confusing, and the patterns they create in our lives can become almost addictive. Some divorcing parents get so emotionally strung out that they are totally overwhelmed by a diverse set of feelings. They don't know which of the many emotions to respond to, and they lose their sense of how to act appropriately in even the most basic situations. Other parents become emotionally preoccupied with their former spouse. When emotions such as anger, fear, or jealousy run extraordinarily high, former spouses may engage in a wide range of destructive behaviors, such as tapping one another's telephones, following the other person, or engaging in other harassing behaviors.

Emotional Coping Responses. Most experts define emotional health as being able to experience and express a wide range of feelings. Although we heartily agree, it is important to keep at least one qualifier in mind when dealing with strong emotions that you have about your divorce: You don't always have to express your feelings about your former spouse *to* your former spouse.

The reality is that you have gotten or are getting a divorce from your former spouse because of basic incompatibilities, which may have included communication problems. Therefore, when it comes to sharing your feelings, whether they be angry feelings or intimate feelings, it is best to leave your former spouse out of the loop. Your new communication relationship with your former spouse should be characterized by facts, not feelings.

Anger can be a particularly difficult emotion for divorced parents to manage. Your former spouse will undoubtedly behave in ways that get under your skin. Rather than venting your angry feelings toward your children's other parent, however, you are much better off to share your feelings with a trusted friend. If a friend is unavailable, or if the feelings are deep and powerful, you may want to consider obtaining personal counseling to help you cope with this difficult time.

Spiritual Reactions to Stress. It is easy to lose your usual religious or spiritual perspective if you are feeling a great deal of stress about your divorce and if you're working hard at single parenting. Your divorce may have been anything from a simple disappointment to an overwhelming devastation. If you're religious, you may find that you suddenly feel very angry toward God, or afraid, or ashamed. If you're not particularly religious, you may feel that life is meaningless and pointless. In essence, one of the biggest core problems that you may experience after your divorce is the inability to feel centered and peaceful.

Spiritual Coping Responses. Everyone needs to feel calm and peaceful and right with the world at least some of the time. Unfortunately, achieving a calm and peaceful state can be exceedingly difficult for divorced and divorcing parents. If you're feeling out-of-sync with your religious or spiritual life, or if you're having lots of trouble creating temporary peaceful periods within your life, it may be time to reach out to a church, spiritual group, or an elder or mentor who might have spiritual guidance to offer.

SUMMARY

If you are a divorcing or divorced parent—or even a parent with a troubled marriage—it probably hasn't been easy to read this book. Taking the advice of the children to heart is a difficult task. In their wise, and rightly self-centered ways, the children's voices in this book are simply asking to have their needs come first. It is a challenging request, but in the end, we believe putting the children first is the right thing to do. We wish you the very best in your efforts to be a loving, discerning, steady, excellent, and of course, humble parent.

APPENDIX

Helping Your Children Cope With Divorce: Age-Based Guidelines

Children are unique, and therefore each one will respond differently to your separation and divorce. Sometimes children's responses are unpredictable; your calm 10-year-old may begin erupting like a volcano, whereas it might become next to impossible to get a word out of your chatterbox 7-year-old. There are no hard and fast rules about how your children will react to your divorce. That being said, your children are likely to respond in characteristic ways, depending upon their ages. Children of different ages have varied physical, social, emotional, and mental abilities and needs. Therefore, when it comes to how your children will react to and handle your divorce, age provides one of our best guidelines.

NEWBORN TO 3 YEARS

Infants and toddlers react physically and behaviorally to parental separation and divorce. Their reactions are characterized as follows:

- A gut-level sensation of loss
- The impression, without much verbal understanding, that something important is missing or something important is wrong
- The expression of grief through tears or wild tantrums

During infancy, one of the biggest issue babies work out is trust. Infants desperately need to establish and maintain a strong attachment to primary and secondary caretakers. You can help your infant adjust to divorce through physical contact, consistency, and emotional bonding.

For toddlers, the main developmental challenge is independence. You should strive to deal with your child's independent behaviors in a balanced and reasonable way.

The following general guidelines are offered to parents living in the same vicinity:

- Unless there are obvious reasons why a change is needed, your child should spend the most time with the parent he or she spent most of the time with before the divorce.
- The parent who has less time with the child should be encouraged and supported in his or her efforts to have frequent (even daily), short visits.
- If parents share daytime caretaking, either establish one nighttime caretaker or implement "nesting," a strategy by which parents move in and out of the house, rather than the child.
- Avoid frequent overnights with the parent who has less time with the child.

Parents who have moved far apart face extra difficulty. Infants and toddlers should not routinely travel back and forth. One parent must agree to travel the distance for visits that are as regular and consistent as possible. Ideally, the visits should be brief and occur during the day.

General Parenting Advice

- Model calmness.
- Try to establish and maintain a daily schedule or routine.
- Keep transitional objects (such as blankets and stuffed animals) and transitional activities (such as songs and schedules) in your child's life.
- Be a soothing and comforting adult—even during the worst of times.
- Provide reassurance about your love for your child and the other parent's love as well.

• As your infant grows into a toddler, begin setting clear limits. . . despite the fact that he or she will try to get his or her way.

AGES 3 TO 5 YEARS

During preschool years, children's verbal skills are expanding, including an ability to begin expressing feelings. Additionally, the increased mastery that children have over their bodily functions and emotions may be inconsistent, resulting in periodic regressions or "emotional meltdowns." For example, children may do the following:

• Begin feeling guilty about the divorce
• Make strong statements such as "I hate you!" or "I want my daddy!"
• Be suddenly overcome with abandonment anxiety

If you live in close proximity to the other parent and want to move toward more equal parenting time, begin initiating gradually longer periods of time with the other parent, and then possibly 1–3 overnights per week or movement toward a split week (3½ days with each parent).

The ability for parents to have approximately equal time with children of divorce depends greatly on the parents' ability to communicate with one another effectively and without hostility. For parents who are unable to accomplish this, more traditional primary residential guidelines (the nonresidential parent gets "visitation" every other weekend and one midweek evening) should begin at this time. Some transition difficulty is likely for children of this age, regardless of how well parents get along.

For parents living farther apart, similar guidelines as those for younger children apply:

• The travel burden should be on the parent, rather than on the child.
• The more available parent will need to encourage and help children maintain communication with the less available parent.
• Include parental photographs and parental memorabilia within both parents' homes.

General Parenting Advice

- Be sure that children realize that the divorce is not their fault.
- Listen to your child's feelings . . . even though they make you uncomfortable.
- Tell your children something like, "It's okay for you to feel sad or mad."
- Continue to have transitional objects available.

AGES 6 TO 8 YEARS

With the onset of elementary school, children begin experiencing new peer relationships, mental challenges and accomplishments, and moral and ethical decision making. Along with these developmental tasks and changes come new and sometimes more intense reactions to divorce. Children may feel the following:

- Deeply saddened by their parents divorce
- An increased sense of guilt and responsibility
- Beginnings of stronger wishes to reunite their parents
- A realization that they could lose both parents

If parents are living close to one another and have opted for nearly equal contact with their child, then the following guidelines can be followed:

- At the beginning of this period, one parent or home may continue as home base.
- Toward the end of this period, alternating weeks at each parents' home may begin.
- Lengthier time periods away from the home base should be implemented only if continuity with peer group, school, and community can be maintained.

For parents living farther apart who have a history of being committed, attached parental figures, the following guidelines are helpful:

- Travel alone for visits up to 2 weeks may begin over the summer and during vacations.

- Regular weeklong visits, including overnights, may occur within the child's usual community (this can be at a motel, a friend of the parent's, or in the child's home).
- Longer visits may be initiated if there is an older sibling and very involved parent.
- Issues of homesickness should be addressed compassionately, and may require reducing visitation time.

General Parenting Advice

- Continue to reassure the child that the divorce is not his or her fault.
- Never criticize the other parent in your child's presence.
- Outline the details of when, where, and how he or she will have regular contact with both parents.
- Let your child complain about your home or surroundings without becoming defensive.
- Maintain an active parenting role by having specific bedtimes, household rules or chores and appropriate consequences for misbehavior.

AGES 9 TO 12 YEARS

As children become more proficient in academic, athletic, artistic, and expressive skills, the preteen years can be both incredibly satisfying and incredibly challenging for parents. During these years, children may react to divorce in these ways:

- Strongly blaming or condemning one parent or the other
- Demanding "adult" explanations for relationship problems
- Experiencing some shame, embarrassment, or rejection
- Trying to console or counsel one or both parents
- Trying to take over the role vacated by an absent parent
- Working hard to reunite divorced parents

For parents living close to one another, guidelines include these:

- Continuation of school, peer, and community activities from both homes

- Nearly equal time with each parent, possibly for up to 2 weeks consecutively in each residence (with midweek access to the other home)
- A 50-50 split during the summer, depending on work, vacation schedules, and children's summer camps or activities

General Parenting Advice

- Never criticize the other parent in your child's presence.
- Outline the details of when, where, and how he or she will have regular contact with both parents.
- Support appropriate and healthy peer relationships, but discourage (and sometimes prohibit) unhealthy peer relationships.
- Maintain an active parenting role by having specific bedtimes, household rules, or chores and appropriate consequences for misbehavior.
- Help your child establish healthy stress management strategies.
- Provide reassurance that he or she will be able to maintain extended family relationships.
- Maintain special time with your child to reduce his or her potential feelings of rejection.

AGES 13 TO 18 YEARS

Often, teenagers want to get out of the house and emancipate from their family. Although these impulses are natural, most teenagers are unprepared to survive outside of the family. This can cause great ambivalence, for parents as well as teens, regarding how much time they can and should spend together. Teenagers are simultaneously grieving the loss of their family closeness, while at the same time pushing for freedom. Their reactions to divorce commonly include these:

- Relief
- Impatience
- Embarrassment
- Distress over parental dating and parental sexuality

- Resistance to visiting parents who live outside of their neighborhood (because teens sometimes value peer relationships over parental relationships)
- Second-guessing, questioning, and blaming one or both parents

For parents living close to one another, guidelines are basically the same as listed above for 9- to 12-year-olds, with some major exceptions:

- Consultation and solicitation of input from the teenager is crucial.
- The teen should not totally control the living arrangements, but must at least endorse contact with both parents.
- Although a permanent schedule should be outlined, flexibility should be built into it.

General Parenting Advice

- Never criticize the other parent in your child's presence.
- Maintain excellent communication between households, otherwise teenagers will play one parent against the other and possibly manipulate the situation to maximize freedom and minimize parental supervision.
- Support appropriate and healthy peer relationships, but discourage (and sometimes prohibit) unhealthy peer relationships.
- Maintain an active parenting role by having specific household rules or chores and appropriate consequences for misbehavior.
- Maintain individualized time with your child.

SOURCES USED TO DEVELOP THIS APPENDIX

Helping Your Kids Cope With Divorce: The Sandcastles Way,
    by M. Gary Neuman

Children of Divorce, by Mitchell Baris and Carla Garrity

Divorce Book for Parents, by Vicki Lansky